I0182551

# THE INHERITANCE

*Pass On Your Pearls*

*Do Not Give Them To Pigs!*

Written by

**Jill L. Deville**

Show What You Know Series

VOLUME 2

Jill L. Deville

ISBN 979-8-9878998-0-9 (Paperback)
ISBN 979-8-9878998-1-6 (Digital)

Jill L Deville
P.O. BOX 876
Basile, La 70515
JillDevilleWorldMinistry@gmail.com
www.JillDevilleWorldMinistry.com

# DEDICATION

I dedicate this book to God, I am grateful He trust me with His word, His task, His story, and His children. I pray you all fall in love with Him as you get to know Him, and not just know of Him. He has huge plans for all of you.

Daughter of the King of Kings

Author, Jill L. Deville

Jill L. Deville

*Matthew 7:6 NIV "Do not give dogs what is sacred; do not throw your pearls to pigs. If you do, they may trample them under their feet, and turn and tear you to pieces.*

# CONTENTS

Jill L. Deville

# INTRODUCTION

This book is written with prayer to help you with wisdom and understanding, on the importance of keeping some matters between you and the Lord. Throughout the Word of God, you will see Jesus tell many people to "go and do not tell". In addition, Jesus would tell many to "go and tell" however He was very specific on who to tell and when to tell. When I came across this verse in Matthew I have treasured it ever since. God's word is truly alive and active. This verse has so much meaning, correction, and direction in it for us, I will share what the Holy Spirit has taught me with this verse:

*Matthew 7:6 NIV "Do not give dogs what is sacred; do not throw your pearls to pigs. If you do, they may trample them under their feet, and turn and tear you to pieces."*

I was like yep there is no way I am telling the dogs and pigs in my life my business; I have been there, and I have done that, and it is not happening again you do not have to worry about that Lord! Then the Holy Spirit began to teach me, guide me, and reveal to me more about pigs and dogs; that just like humans they are not all bad and we cannot group them together as if they are, in this verse or otherwise.

We must gain wisdom and understanding on what Jesus is truly sharing with us in this particular verse that will change our lives and circumstances tremendously!

*James 1:5-6 NKJV  5 If any of you lacks wisdom, let him ask of God, who gives to all liberally and without reproach, and it will be given to him. 6 But let him ask in faith, with no doubting, for he who doubts is like a wave of the sea driven and tossed by the wind.*

We will learn that sometimes we are the stall in our own prayers, we are the set back in our own breakthrough but be of good cheer Jesus shares with us that He gives wisdom and understanding freely, if we ask Him for it. The Lord teaches us that He sends the Holy Spirit to guide, remind, and teach us. How amazing is that to have our very own personal portion of God living inside of us.

*John 14:26 NIV But the Advocate, the Holy Spirit, whom the Father will send in my name, will teach you all things and will remind you of everything I have said to you.*

Many think I do not hear from God because they are expecting an audible voice or some visual in a dream or a moment like Mary and Joseph encountered, but with God He is heard most of all in your conscience through the Holy Spirit. It is not always a verse from the Bible or a statement about prayer, hope, self- control. Most often it simply is pick up that trash you just dropped, turn that light off, go back in and turn that curling iron off, did you take your medication, call your parents, do not forget to check on your friend. You see we often get things confused especially when we feel like the day, or the circumstance is just about us. The Holy Spirit resides in us to teach us honor, integrity, and to remind us of our access to the word of God and how to apply it and receive it in our actions and reactions.

*Luke 12:11-12 NIV 11 "When you are brought before synagogues, rulers and authorities, do not worry about how you will defend yourselves or what you will say, 12 for the Holy Spirit will teach you at that time what you should say."*

We were never designed to defend ourselves God teaches us that in the Word of God. However, tradition teaches us to defend, pretend, offend and so much more. Therefore, God shares with us in John 14:6 that Jesus is the way, the truth, and the life. Some see that verse and think yes, I will pray in Jesus name, others see the verse and say I know this is because Jesus died for our sins there is no way I can make up for my sins and all this is true. But in addition to that the secret is to look deeper into the Way, the Truth, the Life!

*John 14:6 NIV ⁶Jesus answered, "I am the way and the*

*truth and the life. No one comes to the Father except through me.*

You see the way is pertaining to the way Jesus acted and reacted in the Word of God, our very own instruction manual jamb packed with examples, illustrations, directions, and a road map to heaven. Many know of Jesus, they hear of Him in conversation, sermons, worship and may say a prayer at night, for a meal or when in desperate need. But to get to know Jesus is a whole other "Way". The way that is spoken of in John 14:6 is for us to follow the way of Jesus Christ. To learn how to act and react like Him.

The truth is pertaining to God's word. My first go to was the book of Genesis. I was lost and not interested but intrigued at the same time. So, I started to read, I honestly had nothing else to do and a bible was given to me, and I had plenty of time on my hands at that point in my life. I asked where to begin and some said the beginning of the bible, which made perfect since, because that is where it all began. I started to read there and was quickly in shock and awe of many things. It was like an activation of my spirit came to life. It was like a drama, suspense, history lesson within the promises, correction, and prophecy and so much more, but then it started to get confusing to me around the book of Numbers back then.

I then was led to read Matthew at the beginning of the New Testament I skimmed through the first chapter because if I am being honest, I could not pronounce the names let alone comprehend why I needed to know that information about the genealogy of Jesus at the time. But then Mary and Joseph were introduced, and Jesus was born and from there I just keep reading and reading. What got my attention most was that the scripture I was reading, in its entirety, was not the same as what I had heard in church regarding the birth, and the wise men, but I know God used that to keep my attention to keep reading. Oh and I must say later I did go back to Chapter 1 after reading the Old Testament and enjoyed why Matthew put the genealogy. I was like "Oh my" look at Noah and his grandpa and so on, it was pretty cool then.

By Chapter 6 in Matthew, I felt told off and spanked. It was like a light bulb that activated inside of me. I see myself right now in that moment all over again just knowing there was more. I was beginning to understand not everything that was going on in my life was everyone else's fault, or an attack and that I had a choice in it all to turn to Jesus and I had not, not like this.

The life is pertaining to the life we are given from God in the flesh and in the spirit. When reading I learned from the Holy Spirit that the key to the kingdom was found in the definition of repentance to turn from your sin and to turn to Jesus and ask for forgiveness to be saved. In addition to this Jesus shows you in the book of Matthew, Mark, Luke, and John the next layer is also found in the word "turn" it is the very access to freedom of the flesh as well. We learn we always have a choice to turn from the problem, person, situation and turn to Jesus for help and that is what the life of Jesus teaches us.

The book of James is a short book in the bible that got my

attention in "my" way, truth, and life and how to be transformed through Christ Jesus because it teaches you the reason for trials and tribulation and how you can even consider them pure joy. When I say that I had to keep reading because I was like there is no way; why would a Christian even endure things like this especially if we truly believe God is with us and for us. But again, the book of James put me in my place. The book of James taught me accountability and reminded me hey, Jesus was showing you how to act and react in the situations He was put in so you will know how to act in the situation you get in. You would have thought I would have gotten that in the book of Matthew, right?

The book of James teaches us that the word of God is like your IV bag, or your dialysis machine or your blood transfusion. You need it to filter out the old you so that you are filled with the new you, it is there to fill you with purified water from our Lord Jesus Christ so that you are washed clean from the inside out and have the nutrients you need and it is the blood from Jesus Christ that flows through our veins that shows others we are Christ-like so others will meet Christ in us.

The truth is there is no way to truly get to know Jesus Christ without reading His word. Hearing His word from others is not enough. You need a bond with Him and if you are reading this book then you like to read, therefore grab the word of God, and dig in for more. If you like drama, suspense, horror, comedy, self-help it is all in there. You just have to pray for wisdom and understanding prior and the Holy Spirit to guide you and your bible reading experience will change.

These pearls (promises), these scraps ( the trials ) that we gain and inherit throughout our life on earth are true treasures that are meant to be passed down. Both, yes, the pearls and the scraps are both equal in value. They truly are the best inheritance you can leave to your children, grandchildren, and loved ones that will truly be of value and make a difference for generations to come. The pearls, the joy, the secret moments with God, the breakthroughs, the testi-monies, the growth gives hope and evidence that your family is treasured in Heaven by the most high God. Your scraps, the heartache, the pain, the tears, the mess, the struggles, the transformation that feels like you tossed on the floor, pit, or trash gives faith and perseverance to not only you but generations to come.

Pigs or Dogs are not meant to have that from you. Your loved ones are meant to have that so that they can truly carry on THE INHERITANCE.

*Matthew 6:19-21 NKJV Lay Up Treasures in Heaven 19 "Do not lay up for yourselves treasures on earth, where moth and rust destroy and where thieves break in and steal; 20 but lay up for yourselves treasures in heaven, where neither moth nor rust destroys and where thieves do not break in and steal. 21 For where your treasure is, there your heart will be also.*

Jill L. Deville

# CHAPTER 1

# The Dogs?

*Matthew 7:6 NIV "Do not give dogs what is sacred; do not throw your pearls to pigs. If you do, they may trample them under their feet, and turn and tear you to pieces.*

I will keep reminding you of this verse as we read through this book for many reasons, but one specially is so that you hear it when you are in the position to act on it. My prayer is that the Holy Spirit will remind you of it, and you will be activated to say, no this information, this drama, trauma, concern, idea, opportunity if not for others unless God says so. It is time for no more setbacks.

Now we will take some time to consider the dogs this verse may be referring to. Many people refer to some people as dogs. However first let's determine true dog types.

**Pedigree**

Some look for dogs based on their pedigree, statue, titles, and bloodline. The reason for this most often is for breeding purposes to have the best quality looks, breeds, bloodlines. Some owners are not that interested in being friends or associating much with this dog because they just want what they have to offer. Most often they are kept in training, and in kennels to stay well groomed, and know who their owner is and when to listen to them. They are taken out for shows, and performance and then put back into their kennel until the next event, training, or grooming. While others consume their lives with them as their most prized possession.

With that being said, can you relate to these dogs? Do you feel like you are only chosen due to your looks, name, position, money, bloodline? Are maybe this is the type of dog you look for in friends, relationships, coworkers, and you become so consumed with them, or yourself to fit their image of you that you do not realize it?

*Luke 16:21 NKJV 21 desiring to be fed with [a]the crumbs which fell from the rich man's table. Moreover, the dogs came and licked his sores.*

You see many of us want to be in the mist of people like this because we feel less than them and if we can just get close enough maybe just maybe they will spare what they do not want or need to us. Some believe if they are known to associate, marry, work for or date people like this that we will carry on that person's reputation that they worked for or are known for without having to put in the effort themselves, but never realize the wasted effort they put in to be or to be around these people. Some pedigree dogs simply are breed only with their breed and a huge deal is made when they mix that breed with another breed or status.

We must get down to the why we want to be around a person, what is our root reason. We must ask why we are so demanding of our likes, approval and ways for ourselves or our children. Is it pure or is it for our own benefit. The reason God is speaking to you about not giving your scraps to dogs in a situation such as this, is because you will easily become someone's god, or easily chase after someone as though they are our god. They will go to you, they will follow you, they will do anything for you to get what they want from you, meanwhile you will do the same once you see that is what they are there for. If you on the other side of that then you will go to them, and they are all you will think of and want to please.

You both will feel trapped in cages only waiting to be presenting in need, or to show off what you can offer. You will not truly be loved, or respected. I see this so much with influencers, actors, actresses, singers, business owners and so on lately. They wear themselves out day and night and have thousands, or millions of followers but have no clue who truly cares for them, or who is truly there for the scraps. They begin to feel so alone, some get so depressed, they find it had to socialize in person with 1 person when they have millions online following them on social media. You see how evil the devil is with our minds. Some get addicted, some chase the dream with more work, sex, drugs, shopping but it never fills that void. They feel like they are so known, but so un-known. They have no privacy, or time truly private. My heart hearts for them because I know all they want is to know if they are doing good enough, if they are truly loved, who are they truly reaching, or when will they be replaced by the newcomer.

If we are blessed with a position of high status in this world God's word teaches us it is harder for us to get to heaven. He does not say it is impossible. He does not say all rich and popular people of the world will not go to heaven, let's make this clear.

*Mark 10:25 NKJV 25 It is easier for a camel to go through the eye of a needle than for a rich man to enter the kingdom of God."*

God simply says it is easier. Why? Because of all the people, all the dogs seeking scraps. If you choose to give them all your scraps for the wrong reason you will become distracted in your mind, mouth, and motives. If you begin to think more highly of yourselves then guess what, you feel like you are a god to them and you are failing at the blessing you have been given.

Many do not comprehend the gift of success, talent, high achievements in education, medicine, socially or otherwise is a huge honor from God. It means He trust you to serve His people on a high level, with a huge platform. Therefore, you must comprehend if you not using that huge blessing, and platform for Him then there is only one other you doing it for and you need to face that truth about yourself!

# THE INHERITANCE

*Luke 9:26 NKJV 26 For whoever is ashamed of Me and My words, of him the Son of Man will be ashamed when He comes in His own glory, and in His Father's, and of the holy angels.*

Once we decide to act in faith by saying I will follow God and lead others to God no matter what. Then that emptiness you are feeling will go away, that worry, doubt, fear will begin to terminate and be filled with joy, peace, love, self-control. No matter if you the dog in this scenario looking to get what you can by following, working, wanting, needing the best of the best or you have been born in, worked for, or driven to that place to be the dog with the high pedigree; if you have lack of faith, then you have nothing. How can you tell? If you feel you need or must have one another to succeed. All we need is God, He will fill in the true people, places, and things as we seek Him first. He will reach into our heart's desires, and we will use the blessings He gives us for value and honor. Do not give dogs what is sacred. Give your time, love, attention to God and He in turn will bless you abundantly. You can only show this in your actions and reactions without the Buts!

Always remember if you are a child of God, you have the highest pedigree, position, job title, and bloodline. Do not be deceived by the devil. Look back to Matthew 4 when Jesus was being tempted by the devil to relate that you have it all, already too. You just must access it with faith.

We are not meant to lock ourselves in cages in life feeling trapped or unloved just to be important, or honored, or respected. No matter if we on top or the person that desires to serve the one on top in the world. We are meant to be free. God has a plan, and we all have a purpose. Do not stall your purpose with looking for scraps. Do not stall your purpose with giving scraps. Give your all in all of it to God.

**Pets**

Some choose a dog for a companion, a friend, someone to love on them because they are alone, love pets, or simply have a family dog. These type of dogs are lovable, they are fun, they will follow you wherever you go, unless they have done something wrong then they may hide or tell on themselves with their position of their head or tale, some will run away from you, or sit there with the toy, shoe or new toilet paper roll just out of reach with that look , like I have done nothing or please forgive me even though this seems like a million pieces.

What happens to these loving, kindhearted, loyal dogs if you start to give them your scraps when they are on dog food. They will beg for it when you eating, right? They will stop eating their own food that makes them healthy, right? They will start looking to you whenever you in an area that food may come from, and the show begins to get what they want. In addition, they will follow you anywhere you go no matter if it is dangerous or not. They will sit around with you when you sick, and they will comfort you when they know you are upset as long as it takes.

We do not need dogs in our lives that are there to only get our scraps, to only listen to our way, truth, life. What if our way, truth, and life is jamb packed with tradition, sin, and religious works. What if we get so much love from our friend, dog, spouse when we sick, or upset that we do not even consider looking, praying, or focusing on God because we feel we have a comforter already. Many friends, spouses, co-workers, co-Christians and even pets work as the hands and feet of Jesus so that we can feel His love, His touch, His hugs, His conversation. But He will send them. If your first thought is to run to them with your scraps ( injury, pain, concern, circumstance ) then you just selected them over God.

Those dogs will become a distraction, an idol, a god, a setback. You may think no way, they there for me when no one else is, and you are right! You may think God blessed me with them, and you are right! However, they are there because you are calling on them, not calling on God. You may call on God and He may send them, but it is God's choice on how to help, comfort, and release them to you. You need that intimate alone time with God to lean on Him alone so that you do not have a loyal dog come in and fix things for you, distract things for you, make things better for you.

What if yesterday you were praying during worship, Lord takes all of me I want more of you. Then today things started to shift to help you to be activated in God's word to answer that prayer and in the first site of discomfort you run for someone else to fix it instead of utilizing the power, the promises, the information you are learning in God's word. Do not take that from God, or yourself by giving your scraps to the dogs. Use what God is teaching you to apply it in your life.

A loyal friend, spouse, co-worker, co-Christian, dog will follow you anywhere when they truly care for you, especially a dog. Do you want to see that dog follow you to hell just because you constantly feeding them scraps. Just because you constantly are in need or want, just because you dangle something in front of them to get them to do what you want? No, you want a friend, spouse, etc. to be there because they want to be there, because they love to be there and because they are there in obedience to God, not you.

**Service Dogs**

A long time ago you would see service dogs only for police work, and to assist the blind. But now we are seeing more and more people with service dogs for other reasons. A service dog is trained to serve, to guide, to expose, to seek, to help, to hunt, to guide the blind and now more often as emotional support.

We must first truly tap into the need of service in our lives and the root of why the need is there. When we have a circumstance in our lives do we run to services such as hospital, cops, doctor visits, blind people of the world that will fall for our distraction, people in emotional need that will comfort us when they cannot comfort themselves or that will suit our emotional needs.

If tradition has taught us to run to the cops first, then what is being revealed about us? Does this reveal I will call the cops, do not mess with me? Does this reveal I am weak in faith I trust the cops over you Lord? What happens when there is a true need and you not taken seriously because you use the service wrong? A cop is there for an emergency service so that when people are truly in danger or need then they should be called upon. Many call them so often for nonsense for attention, or pride.

Most of us can not admit we can stop the occurrence by changing the situation at home by listening to the Holy Spirit when He says get out but you refuse because the sex, money, or the nice portion they are when they are not drunk or high is worth it. Meanwhile your scraps are ruining the lives of your children, friends, family, workplace, church because you always have strife in your life. Are you giving out these types of scraps to your family, friends, etc. and distracting them from God?

Why do we praise God in church then at home praise the cops, or ourselves in our actions. This teaches people that we are not applying God's word, and that saved people should act this way, this is wrong. This makes others think God would act this way or encourage this behavior and this behavior keeps others from God. What types of scraps do you give to others?

You see the same thing with people that run to the hospital or doctors with minor issues because they have become so paranoid and afraid that they let the enemy convince them they need to go and need to go now. Or for some they go to be cared for because they not cared for at home. The hospital and doctors are gifted with talents to treat emergencies in the hospital that can not wait, they are not there so that family and friends can forgive you for your wrongdoing because, oh you in the hospital now. They are not there for things that can wait till the morning, but you prefer to go because there they will wait on you, and at home no one will help you. If you are looking for forgiveness, if you are looking for attention, if you looking for healing for real; You will not find it with these scraps. You will only find it in Jesus Christ. He will listen to you all day long, He will forgive you every time, He will help you with the ones that will not help you, and He will truly heal you. Stop giving what is scared to dogs. Those moments, those healings, those connections are meant for you and Jesus. To connect and grow together in faith with true love, and self-control.

Running away from God and to the doctor, or hospital first is not going to set your mind at ease or even help you in that moment. Seeking God first and His right standing will. God says He is your healer. God teaches us this throughout His word. He does not have a but in there, such as but go to the doctor while you wait. No, God says seek me first then all things will be added to you.

Am I saying in the middle of a heart attack or stroke to sit there and say I believe God will heal me, no. God probably told you a ton of times prior to this and now He is allowing things so grab your attention and others. Yes, He can still heal you from anything and everything when you call on Him. So on the way to the phone and on the way to the hospital seek Him. Let Him give you a miracle by your faith.

But let's address the ones that fart a little different and go running. God does have servants, mighty servants of God that work in the medical field that are gifted to handle our disobedience when God knows tradition, sin, or generational things come against us. But we must use the commonsense God gave us to discern it is truly time to go, while I am there my miracle healing will heal others too because they will hear of it while I am there, and I can pray for them while I am there. Then other times God will say stay home and go to the bathroom and pray for healing for your cramps from the food you choose to eat knowing it was not good for you.

Some service dogs truly help the blind, spiritually speaking if you a baby Christians or not a Christian at all and you need guidance there is typically someone God will send to intercede for you or with you. Sometimes you will know of them and sometimes you will not. They will just pray alone or you will bond with them, and you will call on them in your moments of need to see clearly. We must know in all things the why we call out and we also must know that eventually there is a maturity that will take place. That you will then eventually use what you learned from your Service dog that was needed when you were blind to then give that same service to someone else when they come to you.

The word teaches us that most of the time we must become

blinded to see, much like the story of Paul. He was a religious man, he killed Christians that were not following the religion properly until God met him where he was and blinded him for 3 days. In those 3 days he saw more than he ever saw with his sight, and it saved his life. You see if we always running to a person, place, or thing with our scraps and not to God, then we may miss the true message in the purpose of the mess. We need wisdom and understanding constantly. This starts a bond between us and Jesus. No one should come before Him. Are we giving your scraps to dogs or are we keeping them between us and Jesus so that He can truly heal and transform us through them.

**Strays**

These dogs come to us as strays, or we go to them because they were picked up as strays and we do not want to see them put to sleep. We want to help them and give them the love no one else would give them and we want them to meet Jesus in us. Some-times we get carried away and think because I saved, and rescued you, you owe me your time, and so on. We may not ever say that to them, but we expect it in our actions and reactions, and they feel it. It ties them and us to bondage and completely ruins the pack, the bond we were meant to have with them. You see in Matthew 25: 31-47 Jesus teaches us we are the ones giving and receiving for Him. We should not want or need the honor, the glory, or anything. We should simply do it because God gifted us with that type of compassion and love.

# THE INHERITANCE

On the other hand, we have other dogs we purchase, get in relationships with, or make friends with and then we feel we must save the day because they always in need. But we must ask, was the scraps we fed them healthy or not. If you are teaching people to come to you and you alone for prayer, needs, wants as a church or person such as church members, sisters in Christ, brothers in Christ, children, parents then guess what when they need, they are coming. You show where the food bowl ( God ) is on day 1, you must show them where the water bowl (Word of God) is also on day 1, and you best show them the place to make waste (get rid of their potty/poop) is here (in prayer). They will not learn this on day one. You got to keep guiding them by getting up and going to the areas ( God, God's Word, and Prayer ) too. You must teach them, here is how with your own actions and reactions or else they will be coming to you. You will hear them whining for food, fussing because they have no water, and you will step all up in their waste. Then guess what if you the only one they can receive from, you just became their god. You meant to lead them to God, not lead them to you. You meant to lead them in your actions and reactions, and do not forget the most important part. You can lead them to the food and water, and area for waste however they have to eat, drink and do it.

They are not just going to hear the words on day one and know what to do. But if they see you, do it, they will follow you to Christ by doing it too. You are their evidence, and their hope that all things are possible with God. Therefore, show them where you get your water (the living word from your Bible ) and say here is your bowl. Show them where you get your food by seeking God first in your actions as you learn and do what Jesus did. ( See and Guide others to Matthew, Mark, Luke, and John to get to know Jesus intimately, not just know of Him). Then show them how and were you get rid of your waste, and scraps by going to God with it all first. He is the only one that knows how to discard of it properly so that the mess creates the Messiah in you! So that the very manure (mess, mistakes, concerns, setbacks, sin, attacks ) become fertilizer. The very fertilizer you needed to produce amazing fruits for others to see and want to eat of as they see you grow in Christ. Without the fertilizer you can not grow. Have you ever seen someone plant without fertilizer successfully?

If you are one that is hard on yourself for your failures, ask God to forgive you then take hold of your mess and use it as a training field for your next level with God. Use it to have compassion, mercy, patience, love, kindness, forgiveness, understanding, meekness, peace so that you will not become a judgmental Christian. Use what you know to reach more people for Christ. You know what you would have listened to, you know what you would not have. Use what the enemy meant for evil for your good and the good of many others like Joseph did in Genesis 50: 19-20. Do not give what is sacred to dogs. Give it to God so that you can be an example to others. So that you can be the very evidence to yourself with your next circumstance that God did it then, and God will do it now.

Not everything is meant to share and that is what God is teaching us in Matthew 7:6. Do not give what is sacred to dogs because most often God is answering a prayer for you. Maybe you said Lord I want to have a peaceful home, I want my family to worship you Lord when we are cleaning, and I want us to read the word of God at the table together each night. So, this is your request to God, right? Do not go post it or share it with a friend. Do not just go demand it to your spouse and child and say this is what we are doing. This is a sacred ask from you to God because you desire this for yourself and your family.

So why would you not share it with friends or post it? You may be thinking I want to be an example of being bold before the Lord, I want to share so others will know my heart, or maybe you believe or make yourself believe that if you share it you will give others hope to try it too. First always check your true motives because God knows them! This request is sacred, it is going to bring a huge breakthrough for you. Therefore, you do not want to just share it. (See Matthew Chapter 6 on why! )

By not sharing you saying Lord I trust you with my ask, and I want to get closer to you with this ask. Then notice that you are asking and looking at the goal by faith not site. Your current situation may be all of you eat when you hungry with little to no conversation because most or all of you are watching TV or on the phone. You may play worship music and it cringes your spouse or your child which then causes chaos in the house with slamming doors, them going outside or to their room, right? So, by site things are one way, and by faith things are desired and decided to be another.

Now you in the hot seat. You have decided to Show What You Know ( apply God's word ). You acknowledge that you the one that asked for this prayer, not them. You are the one God called on to be the light in your household, not them. You are the one ready for the mission, not them. First notice God did not call them to take on this prayer, or mission. He called on you and you called on Him. So this will help you not to put the pressure on the others in the house to follow your commands, demands, fits, judgements or otherwise. God says take my word and apply it and when your mouth and motives line up with your heart and soul then the breakthrough will happen. Meaning you cannot force them, you best not guilt them, you must ensure they see the love, grace, patience, self-control, and mercy of God in this or else they will blame God and run from Him. So now what? You must pray and ask the Holy Spirit to guide you, remind you and teach you what to do and when to do it.

*JOHN 14:26 NKJV But the Helper, the Holy Spirit, whom the Father will send in My name, He will teach you all things, and bring to your remembrance all things that I said to you.*

Here is an example of what this may look like for you. When prayed up and prompted by the Holy Spirit say to your family, I would like for us to try something this week, they may ask what? Or What now? You then boldly share you want to read the word of God each evening. Do not start with chapters, or a book in the bible with allot of names that you can not pronounce. Maybe first consider a devotional or Scripture cards and make it fun for all. A devotional will read the scripture for the day, have a description, then most often a prayer under it. Try this for the first week or so, then start with an open discussion about the verse and the meaning the next week. Followed by let's see what verse is before or after this verse in the Bible and then discussing that as well. The goal is let the Lord move at the pace He knows they will receive, and not in your haste. You have to start small so that you and they are not feeling forced or judged. This is so awkward at first. Press through that stage. It will pass.

The main thing is do not take what is sacred and go tell their friends, or yours. Do not run and say to your spouses' parents guess what we are doing. God wants us to be still, why? Because if you make them feel more uncomfortable or put pressure on them, or praise on you they will flee. They just started doing this with you, enjoy the answered prayer.

We most often are our very own stall because we want to post a picture or share way too much in conversation. This causes discomfort, shame, or leaves an open door for others to be teased for what God is doing. It also often causes you to feel under pressure like you have to give status reports and work in haste for a breakthrough. We have to decide, do we want the prayer answered or do we want to be noticed. Save those things that are sacred between you and God and once everything becomes familiar God will prompt you to share or your spouse and child will share and that will be the most amazing gift of all. Your job is to keep what is sacred to have the breakthrough. To pass it on as the very inheritance your children, family, and friends need so that for generations to come they will be treasured in heaven, where their true treasure is.

*Matthew 6: 1- 4* ¹ *"Be careful not to practice your righteousness in front of others to be seen by them. If you do, you will have no reward from your Father in heaven. 2 "So when you give to the needy, do not announce it with trumpets, as the hypocrites do in the synagogues and on the streets, to be honored by others. Truly I tell you, they have received their reward in full. 3 But when you give to the needy, do not let your left hand know what your right hand is doing, 4 so that your giving may be in secret. Then your Father, who sees what is done in secret, will reward you.*

As you read in Chapter 6 and throughout the word of God this is not just about giving. Jesus goes on to share in your prayer, in your fasting to seek Him first and His right standing, then all will be added to us. If God wants you to share, you will know about it. Your main goal here is to receive the reward from God and not others. If you have so much belief in others, then consider if you had that much belief in the creator of them. Remember who can do something about everything and who truly cannot. That is the type of inheritance you want to leave to others. The very evidence that God is able by the example you leave behind  to share in your testimony as your way, truth and life reflect Jesus shinning through you.

# CHAPTER 2

# The Pigs?

*Matthew 7:6 NIV "Do not give dogs what is sacred; do not throw your pearls to pigs. If you do, they may trample them under their feet, and turn and tear you to pieces.*

We must first know what the pearls and the pigs are, right? Pearls are your hopes, dreams, ideas, breakthroughs, opportunities. Not everyone thinks like you, not everyone gets the breakthroughs like you therefore not everyone will be excited about your next idea or opportunity in life. Our pearls are treasures from God that He trust us with. God knows who will take the treasures and pass them on as an inheritance and He knows which will give them to pigs to turn on us or trample us to pieces.

Some pearls look like they were handed to us in pieces already, right? They may look like a lost job, a marriage problem, a disobedient child, a financial loss. Meanwhile some pearls are exquisite, and you cannot take your eyes off of them like the job you always wanted, the position you desired, the marriage, home, the breakthrough you just were handed, the child you tried so hard to have.

Picture this jewelry box that was handed to you by your

grandmother that passed and it is filled with a variety of jewelry from items that may appear to be junk jewelry to some, then there are some items that you can not wait to find out what they worth, and let's not forget the ones you can not wait to wear to feel close to her because you always saw her wearing them and knew they meant allot to her. She passed these to you so that for generations to come you would share them and pass them on.

This works the same with your precious pearls you collect in your walk with God. You may have some pearls that look like junk to others like loss, heartache, pain, divorce, sin, addiction, illness, imprisonment but within that junk you received the greatest pearls of all. A bond with the Lord and savior Jesus Christ. You always had that beautiful pearl ( plan and purpose  from God ) inside of you just bursting to come out.

Maybe you felt just like that pearl inside that oyster shell underneath all the pressure of the water, just stuck in the mud waiting for someone or something to dig you out. You may have felt trapped in the shell with no light, with all the slim of that oyster around you feeling like you were just swallowed up but then the shell was broken, and the light came in and the pearl was chosen.

I cannot help but recall the story of Jonah while considering this example how God told him to go to Nineveh and Jonah ran the opposite way. He caused all kind of trouble for everyone in his path because he was in disobedience to God. It took him being swallowed up by that big fish to sit in the belly of that big fish in the middle of the ocean, in the depths of the sea for him to understand and truly hear God. During those 3 days he realized what he needed to do and that only God could save him. I always get a huge laugh out of what God told Jonah after all of this; Once Jonah was saved and delivered, he asked God where does He want him to go and He said Jonah go to Nineveh!

*Jonah 3: 1- 3 1 Then the word of the Lord came to Jonah a second time: 2 "Go to the great city of Nineveh and proclaim to it the message I give you." 3 Jonah obeyed the word of the Lord and went to Nineveh. Now Nineveh was a very large city; it took three days to go through it.*

You must read the book of Jonah it will absolutely change your life. God has a huge message in there that just gives your mouth, motives and mind a new vision on your walk and talk with God. You see God does not change the plan or the purpose He has for us. We do! We take all these detours because we lead by the flesh either in temptation or force of the world and others. We have to learn to take a stand and say no, I am the daughter or son of God and I have plans and I have a purpose and I do not have to follow you so that you will like me, I do not have to run away from my problems because I am afraid or do not feel like doing that. We have to understand all that pressure, all those deep waters create the perfect pearl. The perfect version of us.

We are God's treasures, made in His image and He wants us to know this and show this in our behavior. God gets it, do not forget He came in the flesh as Jesus Christ for you, He endured it, felt it, and was able to show you how to apply what you know by His example. That is the most prized pearls you could ever have, they are priceless. Those pearls are the ones you want to wear and share with all you see to show Him off those pearls are the inheritance He left for us.

But for some of us, those are the pearls we tend to want to keep hidden because of what others will think of us for wearing them or because we think some will get so uncomfortable because we have these pearls on that they will think we are showing off or better than them. So, we keep our pearls ( our relationship with Christ) private, and we think that is ok. This reminds me of the story of the talents in the book of Matthew 25.

*Matthew 25:14-30 NKJV The Parable of the Talents*
*[14] "For the kingdom of heaven is like a man traveling to a far country, who called his own servants and delivered his goods to them. [15] And to one he gave five talents, to another two, and to another one, to each according to his own ability; and immediately he went on a journey. [16] Then he who had received the five talents went and traded with them, and made another five talents. [17] And likewise he who had received two gained two more also. [18] But he who had received one went*

*and dug in the ground, and hid his lord's money.* [19] *After a long time the lord of those servants came and settled accounts with them.* [20] *"So he who had received five talents came and brought five other talents, saying, 'Lord, you delivered to me five talents; look, I have gained five more talents besides them.'* [21] *His lord said to him, 'Well done, good and faithful servant; you were faithful over a few things, I will make you ruler over many things. Enter into the joy of your lord.'* [22] *He also who had received two talents came and said, 'Lord, you delivered to me two talents; look, I have gained two more talents besides them.'* [23] *His lord said to him, 'Well done, good and faithful servant; you have been faithful over a few things, I will make you ruler over many things. Enter into the joy of your lord.'* [24] *"Then he who had received the one talent came and said, 'Lord, I knew you to be a hard man, reaping where you have not sown, and gathering where you have not scattered seed.* [25] *And I was afraid, and went and hid your talent in the ground. Look, there you have what is yours.'* [26] *"But his lord answered and said to him, 'You wicked and lazy servant, you knew that I reap where I have not sown, and gather where I have not scattered seed.* [27] *So you ought to have deposited my money with the bankers, and at my coming I would have received back my own with interest.* [28] *So take the talent from him, and give it to him who has ten talents* [29] *For to everyone who has, more will be given, and he will have abundance; but from him who does not have, even what he has will be taken away. [30] And cast the unprofitable servant into the outer darkness. There will be weeping and gnashing of teeth.'*

God knows from our actions and reactions what we can and will do for Him. Therefore, the pearls ( gifts, options, task) He gives to one may appear of more value and trust in comparison however in truth, God's truth they are not. Your 100 in effort will look different from another's 100. It is not that God shows favoritism to anyone, but He is not going to give you pearls that will not be passed on as treasures or to grow if He knows you will just give them to pigs or treat them like scraps that go to dogs.

In many studies and discernment, I see so many self-sabotaging and have no clue they are doing it. I will share some examples with you. Let's say you were having trouble with your spouse, all of a sudden, they started doing things differently whether in routine, health, care, clothes. Instead of communicating with them, instead of praying to God how to address the change one may jump to conclusions and say they cheating on me, they want to leave me, they sneaking around to do this so I will not know. You start to spin out. You know the word of God, you heard all the main scriptures saying seek Him first and His right standing, what God bond together let no man tear apart, the Lord is my Shepard I shall not want, but here you are searching, digging, following, and talking to others all about it.

No matter what you would find out, and no matter who will

listen to you, you will have to stop and comprehend they or that behavior will not fix this! You also must settle down and grasp that you have access to the one that sees all, knows all, and can help with all. Then you must stop and let God in. By sharing your pearls ( issue ) with the wrong people they will take it and turn it against you. By taking your pearls ( fear ) and acting out you are tearing your own self to pieces. That is not of God.

By sharing your pearls with others, you put your pearls on display for others to work for the enemy to steal, kill and destroy. They will kill your spirit and take your joy, they will steal your information and share it with others, and they will destroy your marriage by holding you accountable and trying to make you feel like a fool for not doing something about it. Meanwhile your spouse may just be feeling older, or that you not looking at them the same way, or they may be feeling kind of stuck in a routine or unhealthy. Meanwhile you have a whole screen play planned out in your head and you are now living in fear.

God gave us friends, family, loved ones as a gift and as a treasure. Yes they are there for us to share with and love on and be there for. We need that person to go to and to talk with, but not all things are for them. Some things are your pearls, and you are meant to keep those things to treasure them to raise the value of them so that you can pass on these pearls to generations to come as an inheritance.

By sharing your information with someone that will lift you up or be on your side is not what you need when it comes to your marriage. You need someone that is going to say, ok let's pray. You need someone that will say ok, did you consider this. You need that one that will pray for you behind your back, not prey on you like a lion behind your back. Those type of friends or sisters/brothers in Christ are few. You must seek God first. You must ask Him to send someone if He feels you need them in that moment. But most of all you must stop and consider you are overreacting. You must stop and consider what does God want me to do or say about this. You must be willing to have the conversation with your spouse and say, I noticed the changes you looking good, What brought this on. You have me intrigued to know.

By sharing your pearls with pigs, you are making it harder to forgive, work things out and grow through and from things as you grow in faith. Sometimes yes, it is bad, and the spouse is cheating and you stuck and want or need that hug or someone to talk to. Trust me when I say, Go to God first. Tell Him you need someone you can trust that will help you like Jesus would or ask Him to be there for you because you know you have no one like that. These moments although they do not seem like pearls, they truly are. Let's look a little deeper.

Say that your spouse is cheating or considering cheating. You have the information and you heart-broken and you do not know what to do. You go to God, and you go to His word, and you know you have the right to leave, but you love them and you do not want to leave. You also know you do not want to put up with this. You want answers, you want to know what to do. You feel so trapped that you literally feel like you have no breathe in your lungs. You been together for years and they are all that you know and you just do not get it. You would not ever hurt them that way, why are they hurting you this way.

So you go to God and God knows you want to work it out, or knows that you do not. But either way you want to know why therefore God shares with you in love, mercy, and forgiveness. God then goes on to ask a series of questions like for you Ladies, is your spouse just a labor, a trash man, a bank, a go to when you have nothing else to do. You rarely want to hold his hand let alone sleep with him or do things you used to do. You never try to look nice for him or try new things with him, it may be all about you, your children, your friends, your church. Let's not forget you men, God will ask you is she a cook, a maid, a bill payer, a bank, a sitter to your children, a personal assistant there when you have nothing else to do. You do not look at her the same you just on the phone all the time or working. You do not ask her out on dates or touch her when you pass by. No, the first go to is not "So it is my fault" No absolutely not. Evil never would win over evil. God simply answers our questions when we ask with prayer, tears or our heart when we are in wonder. But we must be clear where things start, and we must make it real clear that two wrongs never make a right.

What is missing in it all? God, God's Word and conversation with your spouse. The word of God refers to the wedding, to the bride and groom allot because your bond with God should be that special. One of the reasons people cannot comprehend the bride and the groom in the bible is because many do not take marriage as serious as it used to be taken. How can you understand something in the spirit if you cannot understand it in the flesh.

We need communication, we need to fight for what is ours. We need to know we are learning God's word to apply it and we also need to know God gives His biggest task ( Pearls ) to the ones that will hold them sacred to them and treat them like the pearls they are. These types of pearls must be treasured and passed on by example because not everyone is willing to keep these pearls and share them with the proper people as a testimony once the healing, breakthrough and example is displayed leaving them to be kept sacred for a lifetime as hope, and evidence that it is not always about the Happily Ever After stories we all come to know and love, it is more of the Eternally Ever After we have been promised that is the true inheritance to pass on.

You have pigs that are just caged as farm animals that do not get out much and at the first sight of slop ( your pearls ) they take it and tear you up because they do not have it so they do not want you to have it. These pearls look like, I am thinking of going to school for _____ and they come in and say, why that? You do not like to do _____, you would not like this, you are going to have to do this and that and I just do not see you having the time or the patience for it. I do not know why you think you would like this. Their root ( the true translation) is saying, I am in fear because you will not have as much time for me with this, you will be doing better than me if you do this, I have no courage to do this so I do not want you to do this, if you do this you will have to move and I do not want that. Now, does it make sense why they try to take your pearls and tear them to pieces. These types of Pigs think of self and they think if they distract you or discourage you that you will stay and cater to them and their needs or in some way they think their fear is dismissed due to changing your mind.

You would think these types of pigs look evil, like enemies like monsters, or people that simply would not be in your heart to cater or contend. However most often they come in the form of parents, teachers, counselors, pastors, spouses, grandparents, children, mentors, and so on. Some do not really want to hurt you, they even convince themselves they helping you by protecting you, but this is not the behavior of God, therefore you must discern it is not of God.

Often it is the very reason no one will try to grow, share, dream or try because they are trained to follow and not lead but God says we can do all things through Christ Jesus that strengthens us. Know that the thought, interest, consideration did not come from nowhere. Therefore do not act in haste, be ready to pray and do your part in action. If the Lord has not ordained, it or planned it for you He will show you in a loving way. You will see that sometimes the thought of something is to help us to turn from whatever and turn to the new direction. Then once He has our attention, He is like no not that, this! While others you just know that you know and you go all in.

Do not every forget we are all made for a purpose and God has the plan.

There are also pigs that are wild and free in the woods tearing up things and destroying things taking and eating whatever they want and just multiplying their herd. They have no sense of direction in life they just get up and repeat the same thing every day they never want to do more, they strive to just tear apart whoever is in the way of what they want and how they want to get it. Most often these pigs are recognizable. You will see them in people that come against you, that do not have the best interest for you, or that simply come at you or anyone else with rage, jealously, pity, and torment. They do look like murderers, thief's, rapist, gossipers, slanders, fornicators, and they are powered up by fear much like the two demon possessed men in Matthew 8: 28-34. When the demons recognized Jesus, they begged to be cast into the pigs and the two men were set free.

*Matthew 8:28-34 NIV Jesus Restores Two Demon-Possessed Men* [28] *When he arrived at the other side in the region of the Gadarenes,[a] two demon-possessed men coming from the tombs met him. They were so violent that no one could pass that way.* [29] *"What do you want with us, Son of God?" they shouted. "Have you come here to torture us before the appointed time?"* [30] *Some distance from them a large herd of pigs was feeding.* [31] *The demons begged Jesus, "If you drive us out, send us into the herd of pigs."* [32] *He said to them, "Go!" So they came out and went into the pigs, and the whole herd rushed down the steep bank into the lake and died in the water. ³³ Those tending the pigs ran off, went into the town and reported all this, including what had happened to the demon-possessed men. ³⁴ Then the whole town went out to meet Jesus. And when they saw him, they pleaded with him to leave their region.*

These types of pigs also come in cute packages like little grandmothers, grandfathers, well known men, and women of authority as bosses, preachers, teachers, loved ones, they come as our children, grandchildren, parents or in the mirror. But the good thing about these type pigs, they recognize God's power and authority and stay away from it. You will notice their body language change as quickly as their words when you take a stance in the Lord's power and authority and say no. Why is that? Because they feel the anointing on you and it makes them fear being around you because they feel God, this is a good thing. It does not mean they hate you or fear you. They just can recognize the anointing and know if they stick around you will rebuke it out of them.

Deep down in them they want that and need that however the legion or spirit that has attached to them, is trying to convince them otherwise. You have to fight for them in prayer, rebuke and fasting to access God's power and authority over them. When you see them trying to stay away from you, this is an amazing thing. It means they still have hope and a chance to be saved and set free. It also means the legion or spirit recognizes your power and authority in Jesus and has to flea when you call it out. Just like Jesus shared in these verses.

It is when they have no fear for God, and no respect for God that you have to be concerned. This is a clear sign they have made their choice and God has cut them off from you to protect you. When someone is not in obedience of God or a child of God they are operating for the enemy. They know that they have no power over God or His children therefore they tread lightly or not at all around you. Because they know when you say get out, they got to go. We must know our access and how to use it, it is the best weapon against the enemy.

So many fear this part of being a Christian because the thought of angels and demons among us let alone in us freaks them out, or seems impossible. This is why you must read the word of God to gain wisdom and understanding in all areas of your walk with God. Not just some. Some fear this part of their walk with God because like I said some come in packages that are loved ones and we want to show mercy, grace, love, forgiveness, and we not wrong to act on our fruits ( Galatians 5:22-23 ) of the spirit ( 1 Corinthians 12: 1-11). However we are completely ignoring our gifts of the spirit that teaches us to get pray and get away. God does not ever want us tormented daily, manipulated, abused, or attacked. That is why He sent His son to teach us and free us with His promises and that is why He sent the Holy Spirit to guide, teach, and remind us what to do and when to do it. Our very own private A. I except this one is all-knowing intelligence not artificially intel-igence. We get those gut feelings, and we know we should not walk there, go there, stay there, do that and we do not listen because we intrigued by the flesh.

God does not want these pigs to have our pearls. He says if you going to take what I give you that is precious to me and tear it up, then I am not giving it to you yet, until you are ready. You ever had someone pass away and their will or words were at this age you will get this car, account, home, jewelry. It is because they have determined it will be more likely that they would be mature enough at that time to receive it and use it for the purpose it was meant for or to carry it on to others as an inheritance to grow like the men with the talents in the parable we just spoke of.

Just because God gave one 10, 5 and 1 they truly each got equal value. You may think well no it was 10, 5  and 1 but in that time of their lives the 10 was 100 % to the one man where the 5 and the 1 was 100 % to the others. God teaches us in Romans 9 how he gives to whom he wants to give because He is God. He also reminds us in James 4 we do not have because we do not ask or we ask with the wrong motives. We must not only learn our scriptures, but it is also important we learn how to access and use them. That is the true inheritance to pass on.

If your child sees you cleaning, working on a car, or with a set work ethic later in life when you visit that child or as that child starts to grow you will see they do many things like you. Most of those things consist of things you do not say, "do this, this way" and "you should do this, that way". I am talking about the action you put behind cooking, cleaning, sports, exercising, or cutting the yard that set routine, they see and repeat it. From your action, from your ways. It is what we pass on in our actions and reactions ( those pearls ) that truly get passed on as the great inheritance. Make sure they are Godly things so that those things of God just come naturally to them. Do not give those pearls to pigs with rage, anger, pity, and fits. Give them the good pearls that they will give from generation to generation as the best inheritance.

# CHAPTER 3

# In Christ?

*Matthew 7:6 NIV "Do not give dogs what is sacred; do not throw your pearls to pigs. If you do, they may trample them under their feet, and turn and tear you to pieces.*

By now I am certain this verse has given you a whole new perspective that will allow you to know how much you are treasured by our Lord and Savior, Jesus Christ. In addition, you may have a new perspective, I pray on how to act and react in regards to the things in your life both good and bad that are meant to be between you and God. That not everything is meant to be share before or while going through it.

*Matthew 6:19-21NIV Treasures in Heaven *19* "Do not store up for yourselves treasures on earth, where moths and vermin destroy, and where thieves break in and steal. *20* But store up for yourselves treasures in heaven, where moths and vermin do not destroy, and where thieves do not break in and steal. *21* For where your treasure is, there your heart will be also.*

When we decide to store our treasures in heaven life changes for us. We begin to not only look forward to the inheritance we have coming in Heaven, but we also get to enjoy that access here on earth. God says what you bind on earth you will bind in heaven, amen?

*Matthew 18:18 NIV "Truly I tell you, whatever you bind on earth will be bound in heaven, and whatever you loose on earth will be loosed in heaven.*

Jesus Christ paid the price for us to have salvation through forgiveness. God came as Jesus Christ in the flesh and lived to show us how to act and react in all situations from being rejected by the religious people, tortured by the Romans ( the law ), betrayed by Judas (a follower) and even Peter (a friend). Jesus showed us what it was like to be tempted by the devil in Matthew 4 where the devil was quoting Him the bible and trying to convince Him if He would trust him he could give Him everything. Jesus had and still has it all. Jesus done that for you and me so that we could not say, God does not get it. But my friend did me this, but my pastor done me that, but the law treated me like this, but the devil tempted me. No! Jesus showed us. His way, truth and life with His actions and reactions. He came to "Show What He Knows" for you and me so that we could " Show What We Know" now!

Jesus came in the flesh to die for our sins because He knew we could not pay the price. He knew we could not ever earn freedom.

Jesus knew religious ways created bondage and we would begin or keep cheating the system like the religious then and the religious still today. We not meant to go to others to be forgiven. We are not meant to pray to statues, rosaries are prayer clothes. Jesus tore that veil. Jesus said now you can come straight to me. You can tell me all about what you did, what others did, who you mad at, who you think you can change. He is saying come to me, not them. Stop being the one to tear up other pearls. He said don't you know you have access to me. You can tell me anything and unlike your judgement, complaints, and fear. I can fix it. I can help them and while I am helping them, I will help you to grow in faith too.

When Jesus becomes your friend that you walk, talk, and want to be like, then you become more and more like Him. Just like the others you tend to want to walk, talk and act like aren't you succeeding in that. But you are not at peace, because you want to know you matter without working for it, right? Be that friend that others do not have to work to have and watch God send you that friend you sowed in. If none fits the bill then guess what, you still have Jesus and that should be enough. He sees your heart. He knows you want friends, loved ones, children, and so on. He will give you all that in right standing. When He knows you ready. How can you be ready you may wonder, or maybe you saying I been ready. But are you really?

Many get new friends and put so much time into them, then here Jesus goes in last place again. Many pray for children they finally get the child and they put not only Jesus in last place but their spouse tearing their relationship with Christ and their marriage to pieces. Then you see the child gets so spoiled they grow up so disrespectful and do not even check on you when you gave your all for them. God will not allow us to be the pigs in our own lives that tear up our own pearls. God will not allow us to be the very dogs that tear up what is sacred. He will wait until we mature in Christ so that we stay in Christ.

Jesus also resurrected for us so that we would know we have Him with us still and we each have a portion of Him with us called the Holy Spirit. That guides, teaches, and reminds us of God's way, truth, and life. As we grow in Christ we will begin to produce more fruits and have abundance, protection, correction, comfort, mercy, grace, love, peace, joy, kindness, longsuffering, and self- control. Others will begin to see Jesus in us from the fruits we produce.

*Galatians 5:22-23 NIV* [22] *But the fruit of the Spirit is love, joy, peace, forbearance, kindness, goodness, faithfulness* [23] *gentleness and self-control. Against such things there is no law.*

*Matthew 7:15-20 NKJV You Will Know Them by Their Fruits* [15] *"Beware of false prophets, who come to you in sheep's clothing, but inwardly they are ravenous wolves.* [16] *You will know them by their fruits. Do men gather grapes from thornbushes or figs from thistles?* [17] *Even so, every good tree bears good fruit, but a bad tree bears bad fruit.* [18] *A good tree cannot bear bad fruit, nor can a bad tree*

*bear good fruit. ¹⁹Every tree that does not bear good fruit is cut down
and thrown into the fire. ²⁰Therefore by their fruits you will know
them.*

These verses will help you to understand what will start to
come out of your mind, mouth, and motives as you transform into a
new creation in Christ. Trading things like lust for love. Why would
you want someone to be crazy about you for looks, money, or sex
instead of genuinely love you? Well, the root begins with how your
pearls ( traditions) were passed on to you. Were they the junk jewelry
pearls that look great for now, that is cheap, they great for a quick fix,
a set look for the moment. You were taught you can pull it off, it
looks real and let's face it you cannot afford the expensive pearls. You
see the actions and reactions of others that play a major part in your
life and you tend to copy and believe that is your fait and only options
too. However, you always have a choice to take that information and
use it, repeat it or change it. God made everyone, and we have a
choice no matter what things look like by site to walk by faith.

Yes, you may have been shown this is and this is all you can
get by traditions, generations and so on. But your Father God has also
shown you that the sky is even not the limit for you when you are His
and He is yours. You have access to all He has to offer. His word says
so. Go read it!! The word of God should have been read to you in the
womb, the word of God should be the best baby shower gift,  the
word of God should be read to you as a child bedtime story, the word

of God should have been your first book given to you when you begin to read. It is your access to your favor on earth and your access in Heaven. It is your very own personalized instruction manual jamb packed with examples, instructions, "how to's", maps, evidence, illustrations and so much more. We need these precious pearls to pass on to generations to come so that everyone can get back to their true home in Heaven. The word of God is your best pearls that you can put on display with honor, that are real, and you cannot wait to share.

When you decide to choose love over lust you decide you want the pearls that are genuine. The ones that will be of value and treasured from generation to generation by the example of love God gifted you with. Do you know what love truly is? Let's see how God explains it to us.

*1 Corinthians 13:4-8 NIV* *⁴Love is patient, love is kind. It does not envy, it does not boast, it is not proud. ⁵It does not dishonor others, it is not self-seeking, it is not easily angered, it keeps no record of wrongs. ⁶Love does not delight in evil but rejoices with the truth. ⁷It always protects, always trusts, always hopes, always perseveres. ⁸Love never fails. But where there are prophecies, they will cease; where there are tongues, they will be stilled; where there is knowledge, it will pass away.*

Now ask am I a loving person and do I have loving people in

my life? This is not to make you feel bad if you do not, we need awareness, wisdom, understanding and hey we need truth and goals, right? If we came to God perfect, why would we need His perfection? We will never be prefect. That is why we need Jesus.

As you focus on love you will understand more how to truly act and react to others. While sowing this love out you will begin to reap this love in. You begin to transform in Christ. The old ways of lust that look like control, fear, worry, manipulation, teasing, pleasing ways they start to decrease in you as love, joy, patience, peace, self-control, favor starts to increase in you. I would like to say, oh this is easy, but it is so hard. Especially when someone is cheating, betraying, lying, or disrespecting you and you married to them, and you like ok God you want me to stay or you want me to go. Then it is like instead of answering He calmly slides this bible verses in front of you and you feel Him say in your conscious what do you think you should do? Did you or do you not love them?

I am not saying this is the case for all, some are in toxic relationships with parents, spouses, significant others, and friends that you know and have known for some time now that God been showing you to get away from, but you stay because you stubborn or you love, or you think it will get better. But again, you not obeying what God is showing you instead you are catering to what the enemy is showing you. In these times you must share with the people God puts in place for you whether they aware they are there for God or not such as law enforcement ( much like the king to Daniel or Pilot with

Jesus ) all serve a purpose and all works together for our good. We learn to ask for wisdom and understanding to know how to look deeper so that you can cut off this bad vine for a moment or for good so that you can grow and produce the fruits ( pearls ) to pass on.

The best inheritance we can give someone is displayed in our actions and reactions. Think back to a time when you were a teen, a child, an adult and there was no way someone would convince you to follow God. Because the examples of God that were introduced to you were not like God much, or at all. It looked like work, judgement, task, confusion, it looked the same as the sinful life you were living. You discerned enough to know, you were not better off following them, and you were right! However, no one ever truly stopped and showed you how to follow Him. Nor did you dare pick up the bible and decide to seek God for clarity. It was easier to have an excuse or place blame. I get it no one ever showed you in such a way that you felt God's presence, saw His actions and reactions in Christians inside and outside of church. You see we teach with our behavior more than anything. We can talk and we can put on an illusion but then life happens, and it is those moments that God is introduced to others as He is truly activated and accessed by us.

When you decide to turn to God and learn His word, He expects you to apply that word in your life not just know it. After all, what would we truly be reading it for, if not to know how to activate it. But many leaders do not teach you this. They give you great lessons, great sermons, they pumped up and you get pumped up and then life goes on. You are sitting there waiting for God to rescue you and think you not worth it because He did not come, when He just gave you the armor, the boat, the fishing rod, the essentials, the road map to get out. We miss it because there is no clarify saying "hey you are learning this to do this". You share testimonies (pearls )to be proof God rescued you and He will rescue them, you hold on to your testimonies (pearls) as a reminder He done it then and He will do it again, that is how you keep track of where you store your pearls.

We must leave the proper pearls to our loved ones so that they truly will access their inheritance.

# CHAPTER 4

# In Friendships?

*Matthew 7:6 NIV "Do not give dogs what is sacred; do not throw your pearls to pigs. If you do, they may trample them under their feet, and turn and tear you to pieces.*

You may have the joy of having a great friend or you may be wondering why it is so hard for me to have at least 1 friend. Either way we have to first narrow down what kind of friend you are or would be. It is best to know the source of things and why people cling to you or do not cling to you.

Begin to ask yourself or take out a notebook and make a list of your qualities. Good on one side and bad on the other side. You may be thinking, I do not have any bad qualities, or you may be thinking okay now I know why I do not have friends. Either way, hold that thought and take a little inventory.

Do you listen well, or can not you not wait for someone to hush so you can talk? Do you consider what others like or do not like, or do you say hey let's go here, let's order this, let's do this. Do you show up when you say you will, or do you say yes to not disappoint at the time, but then make a "good" excuse when that time comes. Do you call to check in, do you answer text back. What do you give to a friendship or what could you give? Do you tell them about the Lord since you love and care for them so much, or would you? Do you remain silent or would you remain silent because you do not want them to stay away from you because of Jesus? Ask would I let this friend come between me and Jesus, have I let this friend come between me and Jesus or is it me, Jesus and my friend? Is the friendship all about their wants and needs. Do they constantly contact you with all their ideas and never ask yours. Do they discredit, or distract you from Jesus, work, school, family?

These questions will help you to understand what type of friends you attract, or stray. Theses questions will help you to understand  why you do not have friends. They will also help you to understand why you do have allot of friends or the clingy friends. Now maybe you want to try that list. You need balance. It does not need to be all about you, or all about them. The bond should not be controlling, or selfish nor should it be people pleasing. If it is they are there because of the control or comfort not the friendship. Do not get mad at them just yet, because most often we equally have that in common with them.

Try sharing, or shifting to bring your ways in, and out of the friendship. With some minor adjustments a little at a time you will have a true friend and you will be a true friend. If not, then it will help you either way. Just know that this chapter will give you discernment about friendships do not use it to become judgmental, or harsh. Do not use it to become clingy or fearful. Use it to sow into a good friend and reap a good friend.

Think of Jesus with Judas. Jesus chose Judas knowing what he was going to do to him in betrayal. Most often we do the same, to fit in or just to have a friend. Jesus done it for love. Judas followed Jesus in awe of Him. Judas just had a root of greed. Even following Jesus, he could not shake that root of greed. It is important as Christians to now you are not the fault of someone else failing or rejecting Jesus. We all have a choice, and we all have a duty to share Him with others in our behavior not just in our knowing. Knowing typically runs people off. It is the action of love, peace, listening, joy, being there, caring, reacting like Jesus that grabs the attention of others especially when they least expect you to. What if Jesus would have been so hurt by Judas that He cried and ran. Then none of us would have salvation for all of our evil sins when we ask for it. We have to realize we get placed in these circumstances to apply God's word in faith by an action or reaction, not by sight in feelings and fear. When we do, this changes the opportunity for someone watching, and you. Jesus teaches us we must pick up our cross, our stuff, our sin, our ways and decide to follow Him. That is how He will know we are His and He is ours.

*Matthew 16:24 NKJV Take Up the Cross and Follow Him*
*²⁴ Then Jesus said to His disciples, "If anyone desires to come after Me, let him deny himself, and take up his cross, and follow Me.*

*Romans 12:1-3 NKJV  Living Sacrifices to God*
*12 I beseech[a] you therefore, brethren, by the mercies of God, that you*
*present your bodies a living sacrifice, holy, acceptable to God, which*
*is your [b]reasonable service.  2 And do not be conformed to this world,*
*but be transformed by the renewing of your mind, that you may prove*
*what is that good and acceptable and perfect will of God.*

Jesus did not expect us to literally carry a cross to say hey look at me, I am like Jesus doing this for you. Jesus does not expect us to be sacrificed on the cross for Him either. He did both for you and me while we were sinners, and for our generation before the sin we even committed that He knew we would commit. We like to get mad at Adam, Eve and Judas, however we betray Jesus every day. We like to get upset with friends because they do us wrong when most often, they never promised us they would do us right. We put so many expec-tations on them and we do not even consider putting those expec-tations on Jesus and following His word to reap the good friend or to be the sacrifice so that God can mold the good friend out of us so many  others can have a good friend. Decide the bad will come. You can use it like Joseph, Job, Ester, and David as motivation with the activation of faith or you can become a fool like Judas. You always have a choice. Ask yourself who wins if I do what you have done to me back or to others?

Some are meant to be set apart in such a way that they are

natural born leaders. They thrive if they don't have or didn't have allot of friends because they easily get off course for that friend and would not accomplish the things they were meant to accomplish. Therefore, you often see them have acquaintances that they just see, call, meet up with and it is though they never left each other. They catch up, they happy to see one another and they go on their way. They love and care for one another as sisters and brothers in Christ, but they do not feel the need for the constant connect. They have confidence, they know one another is there.

Acquaintances are great prayer warriors and great at lifting each other up because they do not grow attached, jealous, or weary from the constant connect. Nothing is wrong with you for not having that constant contact or not even desiring it, it is ok. Acquaintances are great loyal friends, they most often will not gossip or slander you because they are not in your business constantly, nor do they grow weary of you for this same reason.

If you have a childhood friend, a close friend, a new friend that seems the best or even a ton of friends that is great as well. Most people thrive with the unity and get more done together. You see God gives us each talents according to what we are willing to do on earth and according to what He wants to give. You are probably already great at unity and bring each other joy and hope. That is huge and that is a great thing. You get the opportunity and the position to help each other like Jesus is personally working through you to help His friend and that is a great privilege.

What you do not want to do is allow that friendship to come between you and God, you and your spouse or the options to get a spouse, your children, loved ones, growth, or opportunities. Remember a good friend does not take what is sacred ( trauma, drama, illness, loss ) or your pearls ( hopes, dreams, testimonies, options, thoughts, time, love ) and tear someone to pieces with gossip, control, manipulation, discouragement or picking sides. A true friend says ok this is happening, let's go see what Jesus done in this and we will pray and work together to get you there. A true friend says that is awesome I will pray for you for this new opportunity or child. We will believe and receive together. I will be like Aaron and Hur was with Moses and hold up that rod when you cannot. I will be there for you I will not tear you to pieces so that you feel ashamed to go back, take them back, forgive, try again or go for the new opportunities. I will be there for you so you have someone to get excited with and enjoy life with that will lift you up and help you succeed. I will be there to show you what Jesus would do, and I will allow Jesus to work through me to be your true friend in Christ.

You will sow in so many pearls ( blessings & favor ) into your friendships, life and your generations to come from showing your friend, their children, your children, and bystanders what Christ looks like in action in you. By doing this you are showing God you want to leave the best inheritance as a true friend in Christ. Decide to be that Christian, that friend. Be the friend that knows their best friend is Christ and the one that is ready to be like Christ.

Here are some helpful scriptures to help you understand friendships from God's point of view for you. It is time we look from the outside in and not from within.

*Proverbs 25:17 NKJV 17 Seldom set foot in your neighbor's house, Lest he become weary of you and hate you.*

God wants us to be careful not to wear out our welcome. Do not just show up assuming your friend has nothing else to do, and do not stay for hours or days assuming that, this is ok. In addition, on a deeper level God is saying do not get in each other's business so much by sharing all, depending on all, dwelling on all, or having to be around each other all the time. God teaches us you have disagreements because you become too familiar with one another and become worn out or divided.

*1 Thessalonians 5:11NKJV ¹¹ Therefore comfort each other and edify one another, just as you also are doing.*

God wants us to know in a friendship we should lift each other up and not tear each other down. This by no means, recommends a friend saying I am going rob a bank and you saying awesome I think you would be great at it, nor does it mean you should shut them down when their ideas seem outside of you or their normal. Be that friend, ask what brought this on, what you like about that, be the one to help them understand their hopes and dreams and how to pursue them. Do not be the one that distracts or stops them.

# CHAPTER 5

# In Opportunities?

*Matthew 7:6 NIV "Do not give dogs what is sacred; do not throw your pearls to pigs. If you do, they may trample them under their feet, and turn and tear you to pieces.*

I know by now you may be skimming over the verse because you may be sick of reading it or think you got it, but let me encourage you to continue to read it with each chapter as it is important to hear it the next time you are faced with an opportunity, circumstance, trauma or drama. It is important because you will hear it in remembrance by the Holy Spirit and think should I share this or should I remain in conversation with God only in this for now.

Most of us have gotten opportunities in life that we know we worked hard for, while other times we are like wow, how did I get this! You are not the only one that thinks this, I know you know that by now, right?! Some have the same thoughts for their own lives while some people, even family, friends, co-workers or co-Christians are like "WHAT" because of your life and opportunities!! They are getting more again, Lord when it is my turn, or they do not know God yet so there they go with the talking behind your back, facial expressions, and insults. For some of us we retreat from the opportunity to grow to be liked instead, some of us retreat from working to hard, because we do not want it to come off as trying to hard, some of us soar in haste and are bold and say you should be doing as good as me or better, and some just stay feeling rejected, disrespected, and ashamed due to their opportunities. This should not be. The devil and whoever will listen and obey him will kill, steal, and destroy, but Jesus has come to give us life to the fullest.

*John 10:10 NKJV* [10] *The thief does not come except to steal, and to kill, and to destroy. I have come that they may have life, and that they may have it more abundantly.*

Many will acknowledge a portion of this verse about the devil but not about God without realizing it because they simply repeating it from a lesson or sermon verses reading and studying the word on their own. We must understand Jesus promises us every single scripture, not just part of it or the ones we like. Here sure the devil does come like a thief to steal, kill, and destroy but the only way he can is if you allow him. You do not have to allow him. You may be thinking how in the world can I stop him. Your ability to choose this day whom you will serve. In every single circumstance we have the option to go left with the devil or right with God. You may be thinking I do not know what way I am going, but often we go left, which simply looks familiar not even comprehending you letting the devil order your steps. This looks like I will do this to get that, I will take from this to pay that, I will go do this so I can have that. I understand that. That is why you need training in the word of God. You need to get in the word, worship, way, truth, life and activate God that way when you faced with anything at all the first thing you hear in your reaction will become God.

It is like getting ready for a wrestling match. You spar, you train, you lift weights, you run, you all in until that fight comes, right? You do not assume that because you have legs, arms, gloves, the coach, the referee, and the outfit that you going to win, right? Same with God. He is there for you ( the referee ), He gives you the teacher ( Holy Spirit ) the armor ( the word of God = the outfit ) but you got to spar ( put it to action ) you got to exercise ( study it to know when to use what part ). You have all that you need to win in life, you just have to decide to access it.

Some things are meant to be prayed over and worked hard for, knowing in faith God will provide them for you. Some of those things are not meant for you to share with others so that you do not get distracted from faith or focus to achieve those goals. When it looks to one like all of a sudden you were a cashier then the next you were a manager then you can share how you got there and give others hope. A testimony is always more impactful than a thought, or goal to some especially if they are not like minded or do not appear to want better in their own life.

You must learn if someone shares a hope, dream, opportunity with you and you do not feel it makes sense to you. Please comprehend that you were just trusted with someone's hopes, dreams, thoughts, ideas, future. Do not shoot them down. If it is a wild idea and this person lives in haste jumping from one idea to the next as a dreamer, they will only try harder to prove you wrong if you shut them down. You need to access your faith in Jesus. Say things like how did you decide this, what got your attention to do this? You do not have to be fake and say that is great, they will hear your attitude and doubt in your tone. Be like Christ. Do not forget you have access to God to pray over them and pray for them. Say Lord if this is your will help them to do this the way you have it planned for them, and if it is not, please direct their steps and help them to see your plans for them. What this does is heals your heart and mind and saves them from allot of loss and pain if this is not for them, or success to be in agreement if it is. You see God may use 1 wild thought to see both of your hearts and to heal both of your hearts. In addition, God may use that one interest that seems so crazy to get a person to a certain place to see their real opportunity. Do not be the one, that distracts that. God is God. I think He got this, right?

I will give you an example. Sam was sitting in the back seat, Sam is about 5 years old, and mom asked Sam what you want to be when you grow up. He said I want to work at McDonald's. Mom became furious because she worked so hard to make ends meet and never could get the job, she genuinely wanted in the medical field she just knew her son was going to do huge things. She began to cut him down and say things like you better than that, and I can not believe you want to work there, you working as a doctor or you going to do great things.  They get home and while mom is changing clothes from one job to get ready for another, her mom shows up to keep Sam. Grandma asks Sam, why is your mom so upset he said because I want to work at McDonald's when I grow up. Being the loving grandmother and realizing he is 5 years old, she says that is interesting why you chose that profession. He said because the lady in the window always brings us joy, and the burgers are so good. We must understand that simple reaction can change our way of thinking and our path dramatically. What seemed at the moment of devastation to the mom due to her own feelings and concerns could have changed the course of her child forever. You may say forever, it was just one fit. Well sometimes that is all it takes. You see God was showing Sam the position of joy and good food first and how it made him feel. This could have started his journey to being a great chief or having chains of restaurants or a small hometown diner or working at McDonald's a worldwide company with great benefits and advantages to grow. But when we take pieces of the puzzle away ( pieces of the pearls) and throw them on the floor to be trampled underfoot then sometimes it takes years to get back to them. Sometimes it takes years to find the missing pieces to our path/puzzle ( our pearls ).

Often you will see some people get opportunities that you been praying for literally for decades and you like God why them?

Maybe each time God is fixing to give it to you He checks to see if you freed from envy, pride, greed. Maybe it is because you asking with the wrong motives like James 4 teaches us, or maybe it is coming just not yet. Sometimes we pray for 1 small thing when God has a huge thing planned for us. He just wants to see how we act and react in the small things that happen to and around us first, to see if we ready to endure, embrace, and enjoy the huge opportunity. We have to be willing to think deeper. God has plans for you to prosper and succeed. He would not say it, if it was not true. We just have to focus on our faith and wait on the Lord. While we are waiting let's show Him we can be trusted with the little, while He prepares the lots for us.

Our opportunities are like our pearls, some become great displays that we treasure, and some are just junk jewelry we learn from to get to the next level to grow. Either way, we must learn that most of our opportunities should remain between God and us until He is ready for others to hear them. He says you will know my people by their fruits.

I am not saying you should not and cannot share what you like with others such as family and friends. I am saying discern and pray before you do, and God will show you if you truly should share it or wait. Matthew 6 teaches allot on the things you do in secret, how when you activate faith this way, that God sees it and God blesses it. You have to ask why I want to share it. For prayer in agreement, because I trust you to be excited and do this with me, or to boost or challenge me. Our heart needs checkups so we can stay in line with

# THE INHERITANCE

Christ so that we do not miss out on the opportunities, the very pearls God hands down to us and says here this is for you, my daughter, or my son. I want you to have this, because I know you will treasure it and pass it on as the greatest inheritance.

# CHAPTER 6

# The Hardships?

*Matthew 7:6 NIV "Do not give dogs what is sacred; do not throw your pearls to pigs. If you do, they may trample them under their feet, and turn and tear you to pieces.*

What is sacred to you? You may not think your hardships are too sacred, but they truly are. Some are meant to be shared in testimonies later, and some are not. I personally have been through allot and can say through it all my heart goes to okay God what we are doing with this. He often tells me hang this up on display, these pearls need to be shared so these ladies will know what hope looks like when you apply God's word and not your feelings at 1000. Sometimes He tells me put these pearls in a jewelry box these are only for your daughters or your son to use so that if they ever faced with this, or preparing for this they can put these pearls on or reflect on them as a reminder that God is able, and these pearls are their proof. While sometimes God says ok put these pearls on, we are going show what we know to everyone.

God will never prompt you to give a testimony, lift yourself or Him while hurting another growing Christian. God rather wait till both are completely healed then show both of you on display as His most treasured pearls He has created when you remain faithful, and you keep the glory about Him and the ones He wants to reach with your story. It is important to realize not everyone is glad you overcame, not everyone is glad you a fighter, not everyone enjoys seeing you get up each time you hit the ground so hard. Some enjoy that you have hardships, and they hold on to those hardships trying to keep you in the past with their conversations and gossip only to find out that they the only ones still visiting that house, you vacated years ago.

Know that when they speak of these things, the only one you should feel sorry for is them. Pray for healing in their minds and pray they will see God's favor over you. Forgive them each time they do it, it releases God on them to correct them, and it releases you from their bondage.

We must learn that the things we fail, loose, mess up, or struggle in will build perseverance, hope, character, love, mercy, grace, kindness, long-suffering, patience, love, and forgiveness. Think of it as a training. Now you know what it feels like to go through that, so now strive not to do it again, be grateful God rescued you, live as evidence of the new creation in Christ, and give others hope. Your pearls, your hardships create a compassion within that allows you to have compassion, empathy, and symphony. Something that you can not get from lack of enduring.

Be like Joseph in Genesis 50: 19-20 decide what the enemy meant for evil, God meant for your good and the good of many others. When Joseph could have easily assumed the victim role, he continually pressed into the promises of God and stayed the course. Because of his choice, his pearls were given to us as a great inheritance.

*Genesis 50:19-20 NIV ¹⁹ But Joseph said to them, "Don't be afraid. Am I in the place of God? ²⁰ You intended to harm me, but God intended it for good to accomplish what is now being done, the saving of many lives.*

That is what we miss, your victory over a hardship is important. It helps others more than you could every realize. Being a victim does not. Being a victim teaches us we deserve something, we entitled to something, we are needy, or weak. We are not victims. We are victors. Think and read about Jesus. He was beaten to death for you and me prior to that he was rejected by the people of the church, law, and the towns, talked about, cast out, betrayed. Then He was beaten and hung on display to die for you and me. So, I will ask a bold question, Is there a Jesus month, day, year. NO! Why not? Because much like Jesus many others were living sacrifices, or bold leaders ordered by God, protected by God to stand in the place for you and me to not have to. They would be ashamed that we even ask for these things because they endured it, not us.  Our soldiers in the armed forced and our men, women and children of all races and backgrounds come forth and pave the way for us or protect us. They are gifted by

God to do so, whether they know it yet or not.

If we made a month of very point or hardship we would run out of months, right? James 1 teaches us this perseverance produces pure joy when we use it for our good not our bad. Do not let the enemy make fools of us. We deserve nothing, but with Christ we have access to everything. Use that access. You are the daughter and son of the most high God there is no one beneath or above you. We are all made equal in Christ. Let's start to show this in our actions and reactions. Let's speak this in our existence and let's treat people the way we would treat Jesus if we knew it was Him, because to be honest you just never know.

You got to be ready, and you got to stop tearing up your own pearls. We have to learn to throw the scraps in the trash when we done with the situation, and we have to learn when to put on our pearls and say, God got me. If you do then your children, and loved ones will see this and see the fruit coming from you and they will be intrigued to try it. But if you show them that you are no different than the enemy then they will keep acting like the enemy too. We have to understand we are not someone's scraps to be trampled on. We are treasures of the most - High God, we are His treasure, His pearls, His inheritance that will lead others to Him because they will see Him on us and in us!

# CHAPTER 7

# With Children?

*Matthew 7:6 NIV "Do not give dogs what is sacred; do not throw your pearls to pigs. If you do, they may trample them under their feet, and turn and tear you to pieces.*

We love to think our children is our best treasures or will be if we have not had children yet. Did you know you can start praying over your children now before you even have them or before they even meet friends, a spouse, have jobs or opportunities. Most do not think of this because they are thinking of the now, and the need.

If you do not have children yet, been trying or know someone that is dealing with the wait. Begin to activate faith, wisdom and understanding into this part of your life or theirs. Read on Abraham and Sarah in the bible and get hope of on when we ask, God gives. We must think deeper in our prayers so that we do not ask with wrong motives like James 4 teaches us. You may say well I want a child; I know it is not wrong to want a child. I want my child, or my friend to have a child I know that is not wrong and you are right, it is not wrong.

Let's look deeper though. If you or they had this child who

would be first? The child, God, the spouse. Who would be last God, the spouse, you, the child? Who would be God, the spouse, the child, you or God? Read it again to make sure it sinks in, this may or may not be the stall. You may have waited so long, tried so hard or had so much loss that when you finally got a baby you would become so protective, controlling, or cautious that others especially God and your spouse would have to wait. You may forget to teach your child to go to God with you or alone, or you may show your child that they should come to you for everything because you are the comforter, healer, protector, provider. You may begin to ignore God, your spouse, your needs or have your child between you in your life, your bed, your heart, and your head because all you can think or desire is that baby no matter how hungry, tired or lonely you get.

You cannot lose who you are, moms and dads. You can not get caught up in making sure they have the best shoes, options, schools, clothes, home, events, birthdays and rooms without making sure your children have their God!. They need to know the want and need of Jesus Christ. They need to seek Him first and they need to see you seek Jesus first or else they will not believe or receive it. You know how many gather-like cattle in and out of churches each week out of religion, tradition or simply because they feel they are supposed to go.

Most people do not have any idea why they may or may not feel something while they at church. Most go right back into the world with little to no change or desire to truly know Jesus. Sure, they know of Him, sure everyone one saw their cute outfits, sure everyone saw you roll up in your new or clean ride. But why did you truly go to church. Most go for them-selves. The performance, and the interactions. They do not know to go to meet and feel Jesus in unity at all. When they do good deeds, they look at both hands wanting everyone to see and acknowledge them, not God. They are lost more than the bum under the bridge that speaks to Jesus each night. We must know what we are doing and why.

If you can go to a stadium or your living room and jump and yell for your favorite team and show your children that, did you notice your child will repeat it because you do it? If you wake up each day and clean, and do things a set way don't you see your child repeat that? Do you see that they are not following God correctly because no one lead them to Him correctly? Is God waiting on us to get it together then give? You may say well why does this one and that one pop them out like rabbits? You will have to ask God that. That is not our business. God has plans for each of us. Plans for a hope and a future. I believe allot of times it is the ones God trust the most, that waits a little longer because He wants to ensure the best bond, and relationship for those families because He knows you will give them the pearls, you will pass on the best inheritance and that is Jesus Christ and how to apply His word in their life.

What about us mom and dads with children already maybe you were loss then found so you trying to figure out how do I lead my child to Christ when I was a mess prior to this. The answer is, walk by faith not by site. The answer is to learn God's word then apply God's word. By you taking the time to show what you know, your child will see it and have the choice to follow.

We are growing up daily too. We are learning so much as we desire more, and we are not meant to be perfect. Jesus has that part covered. Jesus says you will know my people by their fruits. Meaning if you are showing love, peace, patience, kindness, long-suffering, joy and self-control. You may be thinking Oh my, I know I am not showing all that yet or maybe not at all. But fear not, we get to start now. God sees our heart, as we give our heart to Him, He will help us to transform our actions and reactions.

God knows each person is molded in different times, shapes, and sizes. He is looking to the heart to see you striving to transform, or are you making excuses, or simply saying God made me like this deal with it. God made us to produce His fruits, the enemy attacked us since birth trying to change that and while doing so, he had us tricked into producing bad fruits. But that is okay because God shares with us, He is the Gardener, He will cut off and prune all that is not of Him when we ask. We just need to comprehend this.

Sometimes pruning looks like loss or rejection when in fact it is correction and protection. We must realize first we are children of God no matter how old we look. Most often it is obvious how long we have been a Christian and that we still in the baby stage when we are throwing fits to get our way or crying about everything. Thank God for His mercy and Grace.

God wants us also to know that although we have children, those children are still His children first. He trusted us with those children to raise them and to guide them. Just like God did with Mary and Joseph. I do  not think we comprehend the massive role we have as parents is to raise the child of God, as a child of God.

So, when our children do things good or bad, right or wrong we have to go to God with these pearls and scraps and say Lord what should I do with this. Posting, sharing, embarrassing your child to bring shame to them because you ashamed of them, or hurt by them is not of God.

Would you want your parents posting the stuff you have done. I say thank you Jesus we did not have social media when I was younger, the 10,000 phone calls that was made to all in town was enough. But for real we all fall for it because we want someone to be on team parent or have pity on us. We must realize those scraps are not for dogs to trample underfoot. Those scraps are for us to be reminded of the grace God gave us at their age and also to bring us closer with our child  in prayer. In addition to keep the matter from happening again we can correct and  punish privately to allow God to have that time with us and them to heal and reveal more. If we searching and seeking others we will not hear God over them. We may hear what we want to hear, then we may hear the story all twisted because we could not keep our mouths shut.

You may say well I want them to hear it from me, not others. Well, how about they hear from God. How about while you praying and seeking God, that He shuts the mouths of the lions I think He can handle that, right? If someone comes at you and says I am your mom why you did not tell me, I am your friend why you did not come to me, say I went to God because I knew He could help me. Be that kind of example. After all what can they do for you. Just know your side, is about it, right?

Your children, your stuff is like pearls when you build that trust system with you and God and with you and them even in their failures. You build something huge. Stop allowing the devil to convince you that you wrong for not sharing with others, and you stick with the plan God has for you and your child. That is the true inheritance. That is true honor and integrity. That is the kind of pearls you want to share with your friends, family and especially your child. By sharing this time, I kept things between God and I once the matter is over and now look what God has done, you then turn your scraps to pearls and give others a reason to trust God. That is the true inheritance.

# CHAPTER 8

# In Marriage?

*Matthew 7:6 NIV "Do not give dogs what is sacred; do not throw your pearls to pigs. If you do, they may trample them under their feet, and turn and tear you to pieces.*

Have you ever wondered why some stay married so many years like your grandparents, pastors, parents, and you are in wonder of why this is so hard and what is the secret. The secret is in the scraps and the pearls. When you stand before the alter, and God you say in sickness and in health, for richer for poorer till death do you part. The thing is that we get so caught up in the moment, the decorations, the love, the dress, and in the yes that we sometimes do not comprehend what we are committing to.

Before we get to far into that we must understand that when we meet that person that we can't stop thinking of, can not wait to see, that we are so in love with that nothing will come between you, know that this is God joining you together if and only if you both feel this way. Love is not lust, Love is not controlling, love is not manipulating, love does not work if you love 10% or even 40 % of the person and not the other 90% or 60%. You must be sure. We have watered down marriage throughout the years and we do not take it for what it means, that is one of the main reasons we can not relate to Christ when He talks about a marriage with us. We get confused and wonder, marry Jesus? I am a man! Marry Jesus? I am not a virgin! Marry Jesus? What does this mean I am not good enough for Him? He is not literally going to marry you!

Marriage used to be and for many of us still is very sacred. It is when two people fall in love with one another not because of lust, sex, status, money, looks, to get out, to move on, to have a spouse. It is real and it is true. You simply know that you know, and nothing will convince you otherwise. You both feel it.

God has plans for every single one of us to have that true love. With our spouse and with Him. We tend to get in the way of that with lust, haste, impatience and so much more. We also tend to throw it away with temptations, feelings, lust, and so much more. God teaches us do not give what is sacred to dogs. Why would you want to give your spouse to dogs to trample on them and tear them to pieces. You may be thinking what you mean?

You see if every single time you have an argument, disagreement, or see a flaw in one another (pearls) and you go tell your friend, family, co-worker how much you can not stand this and that you are trampling on your own spouse, you and whomever you sharing with. If you love them, if you truly love them you would pray for them, yes even if it is to stop snoring! I think God can manage things on His end.

When you complain about your spouse, does that stop what your spouse is doing? NO! Because you are calling it into existence even more, you are doubting God's ability to help you because you running to a person, place or thing instead of God, and you becoming further and further from your spouse because you are causing a wedge of hate not love. So here it is, you feeling your spouse has the issue whether it is overeating or snoring but yet you just feel for the schemes of the enemy to come against your spouse instead of helping your spouse.

We must learn to think deeper. God just chose me, God just trusted me to pray for my spouse because He knows I love my spouse, He knows my spouse loves me. God knows if I pray and speak life into my spouse and not evil, then when the Holy Spirit prompts me to speak to my spouse about it they will receive it with love, not hate because God already went before me.

You did not put your spouse to shame by calling them fat in front your friends because you thought they were thinking it, you did not say you cannot sleep because your spouse snores to loud to seek pity. You pray and wait so that when God sets you both free, your spouse from their issue and you from yours that your testimonies together will reach and teach many. That is how you get the treasures. That is what pearls look like. That is the inheritance you need to leave to others so they will not tear themselves and others to pieces.

In this generation there is so much temptation that there used to not be. We will touch on lust, sex, adultery in this section. God's word teaches us that if you so much as look you are committing adultery and one may be quick to feel defeated knowing that, or feel that they can go ahead and do the rest because they know they always looking.

It goes back to love. Do you go seek to look, or when someone passes by do you see them. When you see them do you keep looking, then fantasize about them or do you look the other way and proceed on. You have to stop lying to yourself first, that way you can stop being a liar to God and your spouse. If you see and look away, you not in sin. If you see and do not think of this person in a way that is not of God, then move on. Stop making yourself out to be a monster and do not make your spouse feel or look like trash if a person happens to pass that makes you uncomfortable causing strife in your marriage.

Learn you are the one you both chose. Learn that you are in love. Learn that what God joined together let know man separate. Not even you! Stop being paranoid about social media or when your spouse runs to town randomly. Stop wondering if they have sex with people online, or behind your back. Allowing your mind to wonder this way will cause you confusion, paranoia, control, and manipulation and it will turn into to hate and tear your love to pieces. There are to many temptations in this world for you, you must understand and stay grounded that you have access to God, and God has access to them.

If you pray to God for your marriage, and if you remain confident, and in love in your marriage by faith God will protect you and your spouse from temptation. The reason He will do this is because you are obeying and activating faith over fear. However if you choose to activate fear over faith, then the enemy is invited in to kill, steal and destroy. You have to be aware of which you trust, and which one you show that you trust.

You may be thinking well my spouse cheated before, and they starting to do the same things they did then when they were caught the first time. Well go to God with your pearls ( promises and prayers ) because you threw those scraps ( hurt, betrayal, sin against you) in the trash, right? You forgave. When you forgive you throw out the old, just like God throws out the old for you. If you decide to go back to the dumpster and dig the scraps out the trash that is on you, not God. We must be careful not to let the enemy trick us just because they are doing things like they done before. It does not mean they are cheating again. Pray and ask God to reveal and show you what to do.

Do not go to family, social media, friends, or whomever seeking attention, yeses, a team, or war party to be on your side, cheer you on, comfort you, or give you the yes you are looking for. God says do not give pigs your pearls they will tear them to pieces. God ask you in this moment do you want pity, or power? Do you want answers, or do you want reasoning? You must decide what your marriage means to you. You must understand what your faith means to you. Then you must decide will you show what they mean to you in action. Matthew Chapter 6 will help you allot in this area. It teaches allot about what you do in secret with God, He sees, and He rewards however if you choose to share with others then that is all the reward you will have that they see and give to you. So ask, do I want their pity, comfort, support, yes, cheers or do I want to access power and authority from Jesus Christ?

Again, if you are being beaten, raped, forced, or abused mentally, physically, or verbally do not keep this a secret. God put warning signs within you to stay away to begin with that you did not listen to, and He also put people around you that HE will work through to get you to safety. But yes, seek Him first even in that because He will send you to the people, places and things that will truly help you and so that it does not just feel like a Band-Aid, ok? You need to have a Christian mindset and when you get that, you will be healed. Not everyone is there to help and guide you in the right direction. Some are there to hurt you more, distract you, or think they helping but they are becoming a god to you. You do not need none of that. You have God and you can access God. So, ask Him to help you. Say Lord I have gotten myself into this mess, I love this person and they are hurting me, using me, betraying me and I do not feel like I have options. I do not want to go, but I know I need to. I have no idea where to go, but I know I need to. Will you please reach out to your people around me and share with me who will help me keep my eyes fixed on you, who will help me get to safety and who will help me to get things in order to not live off of them, but to rely on you and do my part.

Begin to pray with wisdom, not for a rescue for your healer

and protector say things like Lord, I need you. I do not want to need this person. I need you to give me the opportunity to leave without fear. I need you to give me a safe place so they will not come around me, and I do not want to feel worse in this place. I want to do my part. Power me up to do my part in Jesus' name amen.

You may be thinking that is allot to pray, that for one is an example however the repetition for decades, hours, days of you saying I do not know what to do is far greater than that and that is what you see, right? The not knowing. So, if you access the all knowing then guess what? That will happen as well. You have your own proof what you say will come. Therefore, use it for your good this time and stop tearing your pearls to pieces.

Now let's talk of the possibility of who you are as a spouse. Are you causing your spouse to feel belittled, like a maid, a handy man, like a sex toy, like they not sexy to you at all, do you give them attention, do you still take them out, do you ask their opinion, do you boss them around, do you care what they want or need. In turn does your spouse do or consider this of you.

Adultery, and Divorce do not happen overnight. It happens with 1 little denial, defense, offense, rejection, and grows one at a time. We must realize in a marriage we are now supposed to operate as one. In order to have the long loving relationships we have to consider each other. Start simple with, do you want to go out to eat it does not matter if you the husband or the wife. Purchase a little snack, flower, item you know they like or looked at but would not get it for themselves or maybe that they forgot they liked due to life. Maybe that item is a little candy you used to eat while dating or a set flower you put in her hair one night. Keep the love alive and active.

Think back to what I would do right now if I had to start dating again and do that with your spouse. Touch them when you walk by, compliment them when you see they trying to look nice, ask if they need help with something they working on, ask if they want to go driving around like you used to. Make efforts. Do not put the children between you in the bed, or between your every detail of life. They grow up and they grow away, and you need to know who your spouse is. You need to know who you are. Give them a great life and show them the love of a marriage and show them their time and what your time looks like to help secure a great marriage for them. Most children fail in their marriage because they depend on parents so much the spouse feels insignificant. That is not how it should be. You are to train your child in the way Jesus teaches you to seek God first, not you. We there to guide and teach them, then we are there to support and grow with them. You cannot hoover over them; they will never feel grown if you do that and meanwhile your spouse is left behind until you have time.

When you have an issue in your marriage, home, family you need to go to one another with it before going to others with it, and more importantly you need to seek God first, or seek God together. If you continue to let pigs and dogs in on what is going on in your marriage, home, family you will find yourself being torn to pieces more and more. They will share with others, they will call bad things into existence, they will cause you harm and not good. Yes, even the ones with the best intentions. Our pearls are meant to be ours to pass on. By showing your children and grandchildren that you have a long-lasting marriage that you faithfully endured, loved, laughed, cried, survived and thrived in will be the very inheritance they need to see. You have the treasured pearls ( God's way, truth, life through Jesus Christ ) therefore do not through what is sacred away. Pass it on so that your generations to come not only reap from this beautiful collection of pearls but all that we meet and know along the way as we share our pearls ( testimonies ) will know this to. Wear theses pearls with confidence knowing we serve a mighty God that has many treasures for us on earth as in Heaven. Decide this truly is the inheritance we need to pass on.

# CHAPTER 9

# Our Feelings?

*Matthew 7:6 NIV "Do not give dogs what is sacred; do not throw your pearls to pigs. If you do, they may trample them under their feet, and turn and tear you to pieces.*

Our feelings in my opinion is the main thing that truly tears us to pieces. We are born, God says in Jeremiah 1:5 He forms us in the womb, then in Jeremiah 29:11  says He has plans for us to prosper and succeed. Let's look at this promise prior to moving forward to help us to access our inheritance, the very pearls He left for us.

*Jeremiah 1:5 NIV "Before I formed you in the womb I knew you, before you were born I set you apart; I appointed you as a prophet to the nations."*

*Jeremiah  29:11NIV For I know the plans I have for you," declares the LORD, "plans to prosper you and not to harm you, plans to give you hope and a future.*

Maybe now you are grown and reading this wondering a few things. One, yes, your parents, guardians whether perfect or not were chosen just like Mary and Joseph to raise you and teach you the way, the truth, the life which means how Jesus acted, and reacted in all situations and give you the information of the bible not only in learning but seeing them apply it in their actions and reactions in their daily lives. How do I know this?

*John 14:6 NIV Jesus answered, "I am the way and the truth and the life. No one comes to the Father except through me.*

*James 1: 22 NIV Do not merely listen to the word, and so deceive yourselves. Do what it says.*

So, this will help you to understand why it may or may not look like you have been formed by Jesus and following His path at this moment. But thank you Jesus, any day that we are still here can be a new day. You simply do not know what will get our attention to finally receive the simplicity of following Christ. You simply do not know what will finally have us fall in love with Christ and have the oh, I get it now moment, but guess what? He knows.

We can not get upset at the parents or people that raised us if they did not get it right or praise our parents or the people that did get it right because all of it falls in God's plan. If not, then why would

Jesus have called Judas, and Why would there be Pilot, or the Giant with David. We all have a purpose no matter what. Some of us choose this day to serve the Lord and some of do not. God gives free will and a choice no matter what. However, He has a plan no matter what! The people, the places, the things like the Giant, the walls of Jericho, the lion's den, and yes even the deception of Adam birth character in us, hope in us, perseverance in us. We can count it all joy the book of James tells us.

Yes, it seems impossible to think betrayal, attacks, illness, loss would bring joy, but God teaches us over and over His ways are not our ways. You see from birth we learn traditions. We learn the ways of our parents from the way they cook, clean, watch sports, seek God, or not. Then our DNA literally absorbs this, and we do it as a natural reaction. You ever had someone say, your great grandmother used to paint, but you had no clue of this prior to your desire to paint, right?

Your great great great grandfather would work on cars without even going to school he just knew what to do and how to do it, wow that is neat that you do the same thing. From the way our nose looks to the way we act we carry on generational blessings or curses and this is your pearls.

When you begin to learn more about the Lord and His word you will find out every move you make, in turn makes a move for someone else in life, in your circle, in your generation. God has a well-oiled functioning system. Just like your body. You ever wondered how your foot, hand, mouth knows what to do and when to do it, even if you took classes to comprehend it. It is still interesting, right? Well for some it is not. They just expect it, they do not consider it, and they do not really care about it. That is until one day when one of the parts do not want to act properly, right? Same with spouses, children, friends, ourselves, our feelings, our future. You get the point. You do not give it much thought until you have no choice.

1 Corinthians 12 I love because it speaks on how the body works in unity. Is goes on to say how each part is needed the uncovered and the covered ( shy and the active ) the bad and good ( the love and the heartache ) the hands need the arms and so on. We are the same. We work as one body in the workplace we in, the world we in, the home we in, the church we in. We have to comprehend although we like the one man show, no matter what you need the viewer therefore you can not do any of this alone. God says where two are more are, I am there in the mist.

Feelings expose our faith. God teaches our actions and reactions come from the heart and what is in the heart is in us. I like to say hey reveal it, so you can heal it Lord. Let me tell you, He does. God's word is meant to be like that IV you get at the hospital. That living water that you need to flow through your veins and  brain and out your mouth and body, to be flushed out from all the stuff that is not good for you.

Say you complain allot, as you fill up on the word with your IV hooked up. You will become more aware of your issue with com-plaining. You will begin to comprehend when I complain I remain.

You will start to realize when a person, place or things happens that you do not feel comfortable with, you were just selected by God to introduce God to the situation and represent Him not the devil. You see God would not complain, therefore you not representing Him by complaining, but by now I think you got that. So here you are this person is just talking on the phone to you and all of a sudden they just start smacking on the phone, and sucking their drink and you all up in your feelings. Your "Old Self" would say gross what are you eating, do you know you smack, that is so nasty. The "New You" is saying Lord please get me off this phone this is just nasty so here you are just listening, enduring. The enemy is saying they need to know this is just nasty, tell them. You are saying well maybe this is God because they need to know. But deep down you know better so you are remaining when your old self would have said something immediately. Then God steps in, the person says I got another call, I will talk to you later. Understand God will send you the ram in the bush like He did with Abraham and Isaac you must learn to wait on the Lord and these exercises help you get there. If you miss these simply exercises, then you get to go to the bigger ones. God has plans for you and however, He needs to get you there He will get your there. His goal is to set you free from bondage and that bondage looks like the scraps you keep picking up and storing thinking you will not have better later.

We must understand this is not just happening to us, it is happening for us, and for many others in the actual matter and beyond that. Let's say everyone at home has a great day and you had a bad day at work, you choose not to deal with it at work with God and the person, place, or thing. So, you are speeding home, causing confusion on the road bobbing, and weaving through traffic like that is going to show the boss not to mess with you again. Then you come home and you slamming doors, cabinets, and you have the entire house is an uproar. They did not do you anything, you were not bold enough to tell the person you upset with anything, nor did you seek God and pray for yourself to act like the lesson you just read on in your bible, you did not pray for that person, place or thing at the time or on the way home, so now your anger has spread into the street, other homes, and your home. First, what are you teaching your child, and others? You are teaching them to sit in church on Sunday and learn then not do. You are teaching them learn about the word of God then do what you want because your feelings are hurt. You are teaching them their day, or feelings do not matter to you, causing them to feel like you feel from the other situations. You are teaching them to throw a fit to get your way.

Since you slammed your breaks in front of one person they now going home aggravated, and no telling who all they will affect. Since you passed one stop sign raging through you have upset one person now they going home in fear that you could have killed them and they will infect their entire household with their feelings. Then there is you, your child went into their room started ranting on social media and started an argument with someone now and fighting with their other friend and that friend is now fighting with their parent.

Your spouse is now retreating to turn the TV loud as it would go and now your little one is crying, and all upset because they feel the noise and the tension in the air. You have to realize you become infectious with your good fruits or bad fruits. You may want to scream right now, but I am a good worker I work so hard and I am never noticed and asked to do more or I am constantly insulted. This is their fault for infecting all of us, not mine. Why am I the one to blame not the boss for all this. Because you learned of this in your word. You were praying Lord I want to be yours show me, and now He is showing you and you do not like how it felt when He was betrayed, rejected, discredited, crucified, resurrected. You just wanted the good parts, or you did not know what you were asking for at all. He says the way is His way, truth and life. His way, truth and life has stuff we got to go through to get their wholeheartedly or we will simply not be truly there.

Our reaction to the boss, saying I am sorry you do not like what I have done, I done my best truly. Try to understand how they feel and walking out enduring. Theses options may help to understand the why's as well.

#1 Maybe that was a notice from God, hey you are not valued here it is time to move on. Do not quit, do not throw a fit, put in applications and pray and let's go on from here.

#2 Let's endure because one day you will be this boss and when someone comes to you that worked hard, and did not sleep with 3 kids and 2 jobs while still giving there all, you will appreciate them, and help them if they truly done wrong or are truly doing great. You will not make them feel like this. We must think deeper. You can not do this in your feelings, you have to access this in your faith.

That way when you grow in faith and endure and bring joy to others that becomes infectious and that is what they see. What comes out the heart no matter how much we want to do good, is still stuck in there somewhere and the only way to get it out is to reveal it, to heal it. Each one of the people in your path from the boss to the baby has a choice to act and react like Christ. We can not use others as an excuse to act out. However, we must not be the fuse lit that causes them to act out either. We must be the light in the darkness that says no, if God allowed this we will pray and wait on the Lord. God gave us feelings, but they are horrible leaders. We must understand we have to follow our faith otherwise we miss the mission; God has just trusted us with.

I love to say take a feeling fast! Decide to trade excuses, complaining, defense, offense, lying, manipulating, controlling, comfort, lust, anger, envy all your scraps that you do not need just throw them away do not give them to the dogs. Decide to put on and access your Pearls for peace, joy, freedom, grace, mercy, self-control, love, kindness, meekness, goodness, faithfulness.

No do not try all at once you will fall flat on your face. Pick one of the least ones you mess up on. Fair warning, it may be the biggest because once you give it all your focus, you may be like oh my goodness I am a liar. Say that you know or think you know that you do not lie. So, you pick this one because it will be easier to start with. You say for 1 day, or 1 week I will not lie. Lord I am giving you my lying tongue. I want you to have the Holy Spirit correct me if I lie and heal me in Jesus' name amen. I love Romans 9:1 for this fast, it helps you to claim it each day and helps you to be aware throughout your day.

*Romans 9:1 NIV  9 I speak the truth in Christ—I am not lying, my conscience confirms it through the Holy Spirit—*

What this verse will do is help you to claim to God you will not lie and ask the Holy Spirit to correct you if you do. In addition you must truly know a lie is just not, Mom I will be there knowing you will not be. Let's look at the lie types:

1. Excuses, I hit her because she hit me.
2. Manipulative, I was going but she was mean, so I am not going now.
3. Exaggerated, I caught a 4' fish when in fact it was 4 inches.
4. Half Truth, I am sorry I was late I lost my keys, but you left out that you slept in.
5. White lies, did you mail your payment off. Yes, if you do not have it by Friday I will resend, knowing you did not.

mail or put the wrong address on purpose.

6.    Hasty, do you want to come with me to
      the movies, Yes let's go. But you not considering if you
      really want to or can go.

There are many ways you can be un-truthful, and we know this, however we must stop this, this form of sin is one we can stop with honesty, and it will not hurt us or anyone else by making this change. Just learn when someone ask you if you want to do some-thing, to say yes, if it is yes and no if it is no. You do not have to be rude. You can just say, no I am sorry I do not feel lead to do that. I pray you find someone else. It is easier than you think.

I know for some of us we do not like to let others down so we do things we do not want to do all the time for others and yes there is a time and place for that as a friend or spouse we must take turns and share experiences that are of God of course. But we do not have to always say yes. We can say no, and we do not have to avoid them to not be asked. Do you rather them feeling hurt because you did not answer a call, text or door rather than being brave in the Lord with faith and saying I am sorry no I do not want to go. Do not say I got to do this or that if you do not have to, say no I do not want to go. God is waiting for the truth. He says the truth will set you free and the only way you can be healed from this fast, this lying tongue is if you do it correctly and truly mean it.

God will bless you abundantly with a massive fruit of the spirit and probably something your heart been desiring because with pruning there is always growth. We have to realize we have plans and a purpose. We have to be healed from the wrong act in regard to our feelings and react with faith in action.

This chapter in John revealed and healed my soul so much because often we want to say the Lord is our father but we do not act like it. When we preach, teach, and lead we need to be ready to show it too. We have to decide when we are learning and growing in Christ how much our feelings, actions, and reactions reflect on the proper way, truth and life. We have to make sure we are leading to Christ by others seeing Him in us and our behavior otherwise we are not about our Father's business.

We are not ambassadors for Christ. Many people hate the thought of going to God let alone church because of false witnesses. A false witness is someone learning or teaching the word but showing something different in their behavior. It is also someone taking the word and teaching their own way to suit their own feelings and ways.

*You Are of Your Father the Devil John 8:39- 47 ESV*
*39 They answered him, "Abraham is our father." Jesus said to them, "If you were Abraham's children, you would be doing the works Abraham did, 40 but now you seek to kill me, a man who has told you the truth that I heard from God. This is not what Abraham did. 41 You are doing the works your father did." They said to*

*him, "We were not born of sexual immorality. We have one Father—even God." [42] Jesus said to them, "If God were your Father, you would love me, for I came from God and I am here. I came not of my own accord, but he sent me. [43] Why do you not understand what I say? It is because you cannot bear to hear my word. [44] You are of your father the devil, and your will is to do your father's desires. He was a murderer from the beginning, and does not stand in the truth, because there is no truth in him. When he lies, he speaks out of his own character, for he is a liar and the father of lies. [45] But because I tell the truth, you do not believe me. [46] Which one of you convicts me of sin? If I tell the truth, why do you not believe me? [47] Whoever is of God hears the words of God. The reason why you do not hear them is that you are not of God."*

This verse among many others feels like God is saying, well if you are mind then show me you are. Please understand if you are not acting and reacting like Jesus then you are acting and reacting like the devil. We have to know the truth, so that the truth will set us free.

# CHAPTER 10

# Your Treasures?

*Matthew 7:6 NIV "Do not give dogs what is sacred; do not throw your pearls to pigs. If you do, they may trample them under their feet, and turn and tear you to pieces.*

God wants you to know through this book that you are highly valued and highly favored by Him. You have made it this far because He has been with you, never leaving you or forsaking you even when we choose to leave Him and forsake Him in our actions and reactions. His mercy, love, grace, forgiveness endures forever for us because we are His when we chose Him to be ours.

God gets our struggle He came down as Jesus Christ in the flesh and was born, lived, died, and was resurrected for you and me. So that He could feel what we were feeling, see what we were seeing and show us what do to and how to do it in every situation. There was not a situation God left out. He done this to teach us the way, the truth, the life is Him. He is the living proof that He is able, and we are able to do all things through Christ Jesus that strengthens us. We love Philippians 4:13, but we do not take the time to know what came before that verse that gave us the access to 13! That treasure lies in verses 10-12 let's look.

*Thanks for Their Gifts Philippians 4: 10-13NIV ¹⁰ I rejoiced greatly in the Lord that at last you renewed your concern for me. Indeed, you were concerned, but you had no opportunity to show it. ¹¹ I am not saying this because I am in need, for I have learned to be content whatever the circumstances. ¹² I know what it is to be in need, and I know what it is to have plenty. I have learned the secret of being content in any and every situation, whether well fed or hungry, whether living in plenty or in want. ¹³ I can do all this through him who gives me strength.*

You see Paul had learned what it was like to have and to have not, to need and to need not, he learned that in all of it joy meant and came from putting **J**esus, **O**thers and then **Y**ourself first. When you done this, you could have joy in the best and worse of times knowing you could do all things through Christ Jesus that strengthens you because it was Christ Jesus that strengthen you during the need too.

Many love to look for the verses that say we can have it all, or as and you shall receive or that all are saved. Those people do not build up treasures in Heaven, they build treasures where moths destroy because they do not want to look around the verse and be accountable. However, whether you look or not the entire bible applies to you. You just will walk around lost wondering why you or why not you. You rather hold on to the one or two verses rather than have faith then when nothing happens because you do not want wisdom and understanding, then you blame God. God did not promise us a free ride. He promised us freedom.

God teaches us in Matthew to learn His word and store up your treasures in heaven. Meaning have a Heaven mindset. Use your hope, joy, peace, love, patience, kindness, self-control that I gave you as gifts so that while you on earth for this little you can lead others to me. He tells us time and time again; they will know you by your fruits. Picture those fruits to be the best Pearls that you can leave as an inheritance not only to your children but to the other children of God so that when you pass this on they will treasure them on Earth as they will in Heaven.

*Matthew 6:19-21 NIV Treasures in Heaven* [19] *"Do not store up for yourselves treasures on earth, where moths and vermin destroy, and where thieves break in and steal.* [20] *But store up for yourselves treasures in heaven, where moths and vermin do not destroy, and where thieves do not break in and steal.* [21] *For where your treasure is, there your heart will be also.*

God says not only can I tell the type of pearls you are wearing but others can tell if they are fake or not too. Why would you want to wear the big bulky heavy fake pearls that flake and turn you colors when you could wear my beautiful pearls and share them with my children so they can all come back home to me with you.

*James 2:5 NKJV Listen, my beloved brethren: did not God choose the poor of this world to be rich in faith and heirs of the kingdom which He promised to those who love Him?*

You may be thinking I have nothing to give or leave my children. I work hard but I can not seem to save and when I do something takes it. God is not looking for you to leave them things like money and material things. If you can, great that is a gift and honor from God not you anyway. What God wants and expects of you is to leave them with the treasures of Him, the treasures of Heaven. The pearls they can wear on earth that will share God's story in their testimony, behavior, and heritage as well as the treasures that will lead them to the pearly gates in Heaven.

Remember each and every action and reaction shares faith, hope, love and Christ. The very narrow path that leads us all to Jesus Christ. Yes it is tempting to fall for the ways of the world with the buts, and excuses however you will have regrets when it is all said and done. We must start somewhere, I pray these helpful fasting tools will help you Show What You Know. Picture you are taking one fake coin out of your treasure box that is marked control but gaining a greater valued coin in gold marked self-control. Often if we understand the trade, the transformation it is much easier to let go and let God.

You see when we act out in anger, worry, excuses, fear, lust we are helping the enemy to be seen, we are helping the enemy to kill, steal and destroy from our loved one, and ourselves. When we begin to grow in wisdom, understanding, faith and courage our heart goes to war for us and others. It wants nothing more than to lay it all down to represent Jesus Christ to glorify Him, and introduce Him to our loved ones, and people in our lives. We begin to understand this battle is never against us and anyone. It is a matter of saying no devil, this body is for the Lord and you not going to operate in it.

God teaches us our bodies are the temple for Jesus Christ. God teaches us what comes out of our hearts is who we truly are. Meaning what we show in our action and reaction is who we are. Knowing it is not ever enough. We must show what we know. I pray this helps you to hold the enemy captive and transform by the renewing of the mind, so that you will know that self-control, peace, and joy is much more rewarding to yourself and others when we decide to activate it.

**In Anger**

1. Ask why am I so angry?
2. Did this person make me feel embarrassed or less than?
3. Did I deserve this?
4. Do I want to give into the enemy and react like him?
5. What did Jesus do when someone did this to Him?

6.  What can I do to lead people to Jesus in this?

7.  How many people will I infect if I react wrong or right?

8.  What are my actions showing love, hate, anger, or forgiveness?

## In Lust

1.  Ask why am I chasing after this person is it love or lust?

2.  Do I want someone to be crazy about me and just want me for sex or looks?

3.  Do I deserve love, or do I feel the need to trap people with lust?

4.  What would Jesus think of me for showing myself this way?

5.  Do I realize this is not faith, to act in lust?

6.  More importantly what is my actions showing lust, faith, love?

## In Envy

1.  Do you get envious or jealous easy?

2.  Do your actions show you get jealous or envious if you cannot admit it?

3.  Do you wonder why them, when you prayed for something, they have?

4.  Do you get excited for others?

5.  Do you sympathize with others when they upset?

6.  Do you like it when people fail because you feel they jumped in to soon?

7.  Do your actions show love, compassion, faith in Christ?

**Complaining**

1. Do you complain, or pray?

2. Which one seems to work best for you?

3. Which one seems to represent God?

**Excuses**

1. Do you make excuses for your behavior ?

2. Does it make you feel better if you have an excuse for your sin?

3. How could you represent God better?

These are just a few but with pray you will realize you cannot listen to a sermon on Romans Chapter 1. Then continue to practice it. It is time for people to stop saying wow that was a great sermon and not apply it if it was so great. Excuses are like gas. Everyone has it, but it is what it is, it is waste. It is not useful for nothing. It stinks and no one wants to hear or smell it. So, excuse yourself and then get it together and decide you will be truthful. You cannot expect to reap the crop ( fruits of the spirit ) if you not watering your garden with the word of God.

Jesus loved to use parables to reach and teach others to ensure they would understand, and when He called me to be a preacher, teacher, speaker and now author I was like how Lord? I felt like Moses I am not eloquent enough for this at all. And trust me I still feel this way, but God shows us the how, the why, the what in our story, in our details and most of all He wanted me to teach like Him. In examples to ensure when you read my books or heard the sermons, or lessons you knew you was hearing Him, not me at all.

For that I am grateful to merely be the hands, feet, mouth, and station that He plays on to reach and teach us all. I want to remain keeping this all about Him and Him only. He has saved me and set me free from so much because I was finally willing to listen and be still. Now I see so many that are in the stages I was in and I ask, how are we going to reach them Lord they do not want to see this or hear that. He tells me time and time again just like I caught you. Now sit down and throw the line over we got fish to catch.

I pray this book helps you to not throw what is scared to dogs and do not give your pearls to pigs. Keep them as a treasure to grow in faith and leave an inheritance for others to grow in faith with as well. Many hear God's word, and it goes in one ear and straight out the other. It looks allot like this. I got a headache mom, go get the Advil after just leaving church knowing you have a healer. No, I am not saying free your home from all medications I am saying let God be the first thing you reach for. Give Him a chance to heal you first. Call your child to you and say in the name of Jesus Lord heal this headache. Lord if she/he or I have done anything to cause this headache then give us wisdom on how to be healed and set free from it in Jesus' name amen. So, what could we have done. Ate a load of candy, listened to loud music, I do not know but we have to learn to ask. Sometimes we not healthy because of our choices. We have to bring awareness of this to heal that too. How will we ever have healing completely if we do not ask and become aware of the roots and sources.

I included Matthew 13 to help you hear from Jesus today and how your treasures come from Heaven and how they are found here on earth as a treasure map to get to Heaven.

*Matthew 13 NIV The Parable of the Sower Matthew 13: 1-9 NIV That same day Jesus went out of the house and sat by the lake. ² Such large crowds gathered around him that he got into a boat and sat in it, while all the people stood on the shore. ³ Then he told them many things in parables, saying: "A farmer went out to sow his seed. ⁴ As he was scattering the seed, some fell along the path, and the birds came and ate it up. ⁵ Some fell on rocky places, where it did not have much soil. It sprang up quickly, because the soil was shallow. ⁶ But when the sun came up, the plants were scorched, and they withered because they had no root. ⁷ Other seed fell among thorns, which grew up and choked the plants. ⁸ Still other seed fell on good soil, where it produced a crop—a hundred, sixty or thirty times what was sown. ⁹ Whoever has ears, let them hear."*

Here Jesus is teaching some hear the word of God ( seeds ) and just as soon as they leave the bible, the church they forget it and continue with the same ways. While others hear the word, they get excited they all in and help others grow, but then the heat comes, and things get hard for them they run and go back to the ways they know instead of what God showed them to do. Then there are others that hear the word of God and get so invested that they judge and use God's word to choke others out and the others run because it is to much. Then there are the ones that take it in with love, wisdom, understanding and a whole lot of prayer and they receive and grow one thing at a time, but it sticks because they in good soil and they grow and produce fruits.

We must understand who we are and who we are for, the word is meant to learn it, then show it. We cannot just know it.

*Matthew 13: 10- 17  NIV  ¹⁰ The disciples came to him and asked, "Why do you speak to the people in parables?" ¹¹ He replied, "Because the knowledge of the secrets of the kingdom of heaven has been given to you, but not to them. ¹² Whoever has will be given more, and they will have an abundance. Whoever does not have, even what they have will be taken from them. ¹³ This is why I speak to them in parables: "Though seeing, they do not see; though hearing, they do not hear or understand. ¹⁴ In them is fulfilled the prophecy of Isaiah: "'You will be ever hearing but never understanding; you will be ever seeing but never perceiving. ¹⁵ For this people's heart has become calloused; they hardly hear with their ears, and they have closed their eyes. Otherwise they might see with their eyes, hear with their ears, understand with their hearts and turn, and I would heal them.'[a]* **16** *But blessed are your eyes because they see, and your ears because they hear.* **17** *For truly I tell you, many prophets and righteous people longed to see what you see but did not see it, and to hear what you hear but did not hear it.*

In your bible this is written in red, therefore it is what Jesus was stating to them then and to us now. We have ears to hear, and eyes to see. We just have to figure out are we only seeing and hearing in the natural or in the spirit too? We can not preach on God's word then party in the streets with the town drinking and dancing like a sinner. Sure, God says do not drink to get drunk and you saw him dancing at many weddings.

So what happens leaders take this and they use it for their own flesh. First you have to ask, what am I teaching. What am I sharing with the youth, the adults, they community. Am I trying to fit in with them or am I trying to show them how to be the light even in this. Only you know and it is no one else's place to judge but God. However, there are many discerning children that see this as a free ride to fake it all and as leaders both in Christians and Speakers we have to comprehend our accountability in Matthew 18!

The question is are you seeking the drink to cover the pain, to fit in, to show off, to express yourself, to have courage? If so you are in sin, and you leading others to hell by showing this is ok. Same with gossip, same with addiction or murder. There is no difference. Sin is sin. Be aware of why your sin is so much more important to you than your promise and promotion from God.

*Matthew 13: 18- 23 NIV* <sup>18</sup> *"Listen then to what the parable of the sower means:* <sup>19</sup> *When anyone hears the message about the kingdom and does not understand it, the evil one comes and snatches away what was sown in their heart. This is the seed sown along the path.* <sup>20</sup> *The seed falling on rocky ground refers to someone who hears the word and at once receives it with joy.* <sup>21</sup> *But since they have no root, they last only a short time. When trouble or persecution comes because of the word, they quickly fall away.* <sup>22</sup> *The seed falling among the thorns refers to someone who hears the word, but the worries of this life and the deceitfulness of wealth choke the word, making it unfruitful.* <sup>23</sup> *But the seed falling on good soil refers to someone who hears the word and understands it. This is the one who produces a crop, yielding a hundred, sixty or thirty times what was sown."*

Jesus often goes back and shares exactly what He means in parables. You just need to take the time to pick a chapter and read it to get the full picture and the whole truth from Jesus. He did not leave anything out. He wanted to make sure we received it all. He left us the greatest inheritance of all.

*The Parable of the Weeds Matthew 13: 24-30 NIV*
*24 Jesus told them another parable: "The kingdom of heaven is like a*
*man who sowed good seed in his field. 25 But while everyone was*
*sleeping, his enemy came and sowed weeds among the wheat, and went*
*away. 26 When the wheat sprouted and formed heads, then the weeds*
*also appeared. 27 "The owner's servants came to him and said, 'Sir,*
*didn't you sow good seed in your field? Where then did the weeds come*
*from?' 28 "'An enemy did this,' he replied. "The servants asked him,*
*'Do you want us to go and pull them up?' 29 "'No,' he answered,*
*'because while you are pulling the weeds, you may uproot the wheat with*
*them. 30 Let both grow together until the harvest. At that time I will*
*tell the harvesters: First collect the weeds and tie them in bundles to be*
*burned; then gather the wheat and bring it into my barn.'"*

Many times, in your home, life, church there will be great crop
and weeds. God does not allow others to just go in and pull you up
until the harvest because He prays that the good crop will encourage
others and not be choked out by the weeds. You see weeds look like
temptation of foods, addiction, fitting in, acting out, seeking pity,
looking for pleasure. We have to learn how to resist those things and
not be suffocated by those things so that we can grow pass the weeds
showing them they have no hold or affect on us. You see if Jesus
would come in and pull the weeds out of our life too soon like people,

places or things He just may grab us up too with them because we may not be ready yet to let go. He knows this. Thank God, that God has more patience than we have with our loved ones, members, staff, children, right? But the thing is God teaches us we here to learn to act and react like Him, so we do not choke others out or run them off that we show them how to grow in Christ by simply being like Christ.

*The Parables of the Mustard Seed and the Yeast Matthew 13: 31- 32 NIV  [31] He told them another parable: "The kingdom of heaven is like a mustard seed, which a man took and planted in his field. [32] Though it is the smallest of all seeds, yet when it grows, it is the largest of garden plants and becomes a tree, so that the birds come and perch in its branches."*

You may be like the mustard seed or have faith as small as the mustard seed, but Jesus Christ says, that is all you need. I can take it from there. As you grow you will be the biggest for me because slow and steady wins the race. Slow and steady remains. Wisdom and understanding are for greater than titles and acknow-ledgements when it comes to God. He is looking to see your heart and what you desire.

*Matthew 13: 31- 32 NIV  [33] He told them still another parable: "The kingdom of heaven is like yeast that a woman took and mixed into about sixty pounds[b] of flour until it worked all through the dough." [34] Jesus spoke all these things to the crowd in parables; he did not say anything to them without using a parable. [35] So was fulfilled what was spoken through the prophet:"I will open my mouth in parables,I will utter things hidden since the creation of the world."[c]*

Anyone that has baked if you are dealing with dough, you know you dealing with a battle to roll, knead, keep it from sticking, and repeat over and over until you have all the flour mixed in. Like Jesus said I know you will not hear this word one time and say, okay I got it let's go do it now. But as you learn, roll, stick, and roll again it will begin to make sense and bond together and once baked it will be the best bread others have tasted because they will see and taste of Jesus. The problem is people are hearing of Him, then seeing the ones that speak of Him not act like Him and they having a huge issue figuring out what this means. We have to decide to learn and do, to show what we know so that others truly will follow Christ because they will meet Him in us.

*The Parable of the Weeds Explained Matthew 13: 36- 42 NIV [36] Then he left the crowd and went into the house. His disciples came to him and said, "Explain to us the parable of the weeds in the field." [37] He answered, "The one who sowed the good seed is the Son of an. [38] The field is the world, and the good seed stands for the people of the kingdom. The weeds are the people of the evil one, [39] and the enemy who sows them is the devil. The harvest is the end of the age, and the harvesters are angels. [40] "As the weeds are pulled up and burned in the fire, so it will be at the end of the age. [41] The Son of Man will send out his angels, and they will weed out of his kingdom everything that causes sin and all who do evil. [42] They will throw them into the blazing furnace, where there will be weeping and gnashing of teeth. [43] Then the righteous will shine like the sun in the kingdom of their Father. Whoever has ears, let them hear.*

Jesus wants us to know with our children, members, friends, spouse we can lead them to the water, but they will have to drink it on their own. We are not accountable if they choose to keep living and doing things their own way. However, He does want our reaction to their ways to be like His reaction to show love, grace, mercy, and kindness so that eventually just like you and me they will see that and come to Him and know they can trust us to help them if they need help to get to Him.

*The Parables of the Hidden Treasure and the Pearl Matthew 13: 42-46 NIV [44] "The kingdom of heaven is like treasure hidden in a field. When a man found it, he hid it again, and then in his joy went and sold all he had and bought that field. [45] "Again, the kingdom of heaven is like a merchant looking for fine pearls.* [46] *When he found one of great value, he went away and sold everything he had and bought it.*

Once you find Jesus and fall in love with Him you willing to sell your old ways, habits, desires and follow Him. You realize the pearls He has is much more rewarding than anything you could or would do on your own. You begin to understand that you have nothing without Him and you cannot get to the next level without Him.

*The Parable of the Net  Matthew 13: 47- 52  NIV*

[47] *"Once again, the kingdom of heaven is like a net that was let down into the lake and caught all kinds of fish.* [48] *When it was full, the fishermen pulled it up on the shore. Then they sat down and collected the good fish in baskets, but threw the bad away.* [49] *This is how it will be at the end of the age. The angels will come and separate the wicked from the righteous* [50] *and throw them into the blazing furnace, where there will be weeping and gnashing of teeth.* [51] *"Have you understood all these things?" Jesus asked. "Yes," they replied.* [52] *He said to them, "Therefore every teacher of the law who has become a disciple in the kingdom of heaven is like the owner of a house who brings out of*

*his storeroom new treasures as well as old."*

If all teachers, preachers, priest, and Christians would comprehend our position with Christ when we lead others. God says cast out your net, share my word, show how you applied my word, share testimonies, and let them see me in you. You will catch good and bad fish. Do not be concerned with that, He will sort them out. He is not looking for us to sort them out.

Yes, He will come to you and say, hey address this and share this and in their disobedience or gratitude things will shift and change but no matter what it should remain between them and God. You are just the radio station He is playing on to reach them, the hands, and feet He is working through to feel them and guide them therefore be obedient and make sure you are fitting in line with His right standing and not the ways of the world. Jesus gets it, you feel alone, left out, and less than. But you are not. He is right there with you, and He loves you and He has plans for you to prosper and succeed He does not want you failing in this mission to fit into the world. He wants you to know you on this journey to get others to Heaven not hell.

Our pearls become the people that see Jesus in us and follow us to Him, Our pearls are the ones that are His most prized treasured standing side by side with us on the showroom floor waiting to walk into Heaven. We are His pearls, and He will not let anyone trample and tear us to pieces if we seek Him first and His right standing.

*A Prophet Without Honor Matthew 13: 53-58 NIV*

*53 When Jesus had finished these parables, he moved on from there. 54 Coming to his hometown, he began teaching the people in their synagogue, and they were amazed. "Where did this man get this wisdom and these miraculous powers?" they asked. 55 "Isn't this the carpenter's son? Isn't his mother's name Mary, and aren't his brothers James, Joseph, Simon and Judas? 56 Aren't all his sisters with us? Where then did this man get all these things?" 57 And they took offense at him. But Jesus said to them, "A prophet is not without honor except in his own town and in his own home." 58 And he did not do many miracles there because of their lack of faith.*

Just like Jesus many of us have to reach more out of our home town, town we live in, outside of our workplace because they just want to do like they done to Jesus. Aren't you the one that… instead of using it as their hope that wow if God can do that in her what can He do for me. It just does not work like that. But we have social media, and we have access. We cannot hide; we are not meant to hide. God teaches us to get out there and shine bright. If they think we crazy, he says oh well they will know you crazy for me and about me. There is literally a verse that says that. Check it out.

*2 Corinthians 5:13-21 NLT 13 If it seems we are crazy, it is to bring glory to God. And if we are in our right minds, it is for your benefit. 14 Either way, Christ's love controls us. Since we believe that Christ died for all, we also believe that we have all died to our old life. 15 He died for everyone so that those who receive his new life will no longer live for themselves. Instead, they will live for Christ, who died and was raised for them. 16 So we have stopped evaluating others from a human point of view. At one time we thought of Christ merely from a human point of view. How differently we know him now! 17 This means that anyone who belongs to Christ has become a new person. The old life is gone; a new life has begun! 18 And all of this is a gift from God, who brought us back to himself through Christ. And God has given us this task of reconciling people to him. 19 For God was in Christ, reconciling the world to himself, no longer counting people's sins against them. And he gave us this wonderful message of reconciliation. 20 So we are Christ's ambassadors; God is making his appeal through us. We speak for Christ when we plead, "Come back to God!" 21 For God made Christ, who never sinned, to be the offering for our sin, so that we could be made right with God through Christ.*

I included Matthew 13 in case you don't read the word of God allot. You will see that Jesus wants to make sure you understand His word and how to apply His word. Once you finish this book let me encourage you to go read the book of Matthew then I pray that you intrigued to learn more and read Mark, Luke and John.

Here is why. When you read these chapters,
you meet Jesus Christ. You know longer know of Him. You know
Him. Look at it as reading His personal journal you stubbled across in
this world and now you have all the access and answers to his life and
yours. You will learn about His heritage, your heritage, His birth, His
mom and dad, His Father, the people He liked to be around, the
people He healed, and saved, the people that rejected Him in church,
in town, in the law, in life. You will learn about all the temptation,
tears, and days of joy and excitement. You will fully know Him, and
you will then truly understand how to
be like Him. You will fall in love with Him and there will be nothing
no one can do to separate your love from Him, no, not no-one.

These four books will change your life for the rest of your life.
You will inherit the highest value of pearls they are from Heaven, and
you will begin to put them on and show others how beautiful they are.
That is the most treasured inheritance you could ever leave behind.
Therefore, I ask you to keep your pearls and  pass them on. Do not let
others tear them to pieces. Let your story, and you be the best
inheritance to pass on.

Jill L. Deville

# ABOUT THE AUTHOR

This book was written by Jill L. Deville, first and foremost the daughter of God. Her passion is to lead others to Christ by learning God's word and applying it in her life with prayer, faith and hope that others meet Christ in her and are drawn to Him. Jill's desire is that people would get to know Jesus Christ not just know of Him. You can see and feel that Jill writes with simplicity like her Father with examples and love to help us to be more accountable while sharing that we are not reading or learning God's word just to know it. We are learning God's word so that we know how to show it.

Jill shares that she wants you to consider the bible as a journal you came across that has Jesus on the top of it and feel so intrigued to hear his personal thoughts, actions, heritage, instructions, examples and so much more. The bible should be the first thing we give to someone as a gift at a baby shower, wedding, as well as a baptism or first visit to church as it is our instruction manual that some tossed because they thought looking at the picture was enough to put it together. It is not, this time. We need intimacy with the Lord and in

Jill's books she shares how God will give us this as we draw into Him with a new desire to know and do more.

Jill is a wife going on 25 years as of 2023 and been with her husband for 30 years. Jill is a mother of 3 and still a grandmother of 2. She loves to preach the word of God at her and her husband's church Gift Ministry of Louisiana in a small little town, Basile Louisiana. Jill Deville is also a motivation speaker, teacher and writer for Jill Deville World Ministry. God has attracted a huge following on social media through Jill Deville World Ministry as she makes sure everyone knows, " It is all God, she is just the station He is playing on". Jill writes all her own sermons, studies, teachings and books with the Holy Spirit teaching and guiding her. Jill not only shares what God teaches her, she shares the evidence of it in her life as she strives daily to please, and work for God and His people.

After retirement, Jill went back to school 8 years ago in the law field to be s State Certified Mediator to assist families, people, and businesses with resolving conflict in private with the guidance of God. Jill did not come by any of these accomplishments without huge devastation, loss, and failures in her life however God used every single bit of it to create in her what He is doing today.

Jill wants you to know books like this should be read to get you fired back up to dig deeper into your word and dig deeper into your purpose. God has so many huge plans for each and every one of you and when it looks like you at a loss, when it looks like you failed so many times, when it looks like there is no way you will do better,

God steps in when you call Him and shows you the narrow path you need to take to get there. It has been there all along you just let the weeds overtake it. Rise up and get them large garden scissors out and cut that old junk out your way and walk.

Jill loves the scripture from Acts 3:6 and wants to leave this book with that in mind to charge and challenge you today.

***Acts 3:6 NKJV Then Peter said, "Silver and gold I do not have, but what I do have I give you: In the name of Jesus Christ of Nazareth, rise up and walk."***

The inheritance we leave is that simple. We have the best of the best inheritance there is to pass on to share how to get up and walk by us getting up and walking!

We must Show What We Know so that others have the chance to know that the pearls are treasures. Treasures that lead us to the Kingdom of Heaven to be with the King of Kings, Our Father, God!

We are the inheritance that God is passing on to our generations to come, so that they will know how to get home too.

Love you all Big Big!!

Jill L. Deville

Jill L. Deville

Thank you for your time, and support by reading the Inheritance. I pray to stay connected to you and hear what you learned and like most from the Inheritance.

To stay connected follow us on TIKTOK, FACEBOOK, YOUTUBE, & INSTAGRAM under Jill Deville World Ministry, Gift Ministry of Louisiana and Show What You Know. Don't forget to leave a review, God bless you.

www.ingramcontent.com/pod-product-compliance
Lightning Source LLC
Chambersburg PA
CBHW032137040426
42449CB00005B/284